# SAI MESSAGES

## for

## YOU and ME

ISBN 0-907555-02-0

All rights reserved by Vrindavanum Books, the non-profit division of Sawbridge Enterprises Ltd., 37 Sydney Street, London SW3 6PU, England.

Copyright© Vrindavanum Books 1985

This book is especially produced for Sai devotees and sold at cost. No material from it may be reproduced by any means whatsoever for sale or circulation without the written permission of the publishers.

Photoset and printed by A. & R. Lithographic Services,
16 - 22 Pritchards Road, London E.2 9AP.

# SAI MESSAGES

## for

## YOU and ME

Lucas Ralli

VRINDAVANUM BOOKS

LONDON

*"Swami, why do I not hear Your voice?"*

*"My child, when you are attuned to Me, your voice is My voice."*

# CONTENTS

Foreword .........................................
Introduction .......................................
Part I  Love .......................................
Part II Other Themes ..............................
Index ............................................

# FOREWORD

Bhagavan Sri Sathya Sai Baba, when speaking of himself, uses the name "Swami" meaning "Master"; we too address him so, since that word emboldens us to move closer to his feet and imbibe, as pupils, the lessons he lovingly teaches us with translucent clarity. However incompetent and incorrigible we are, his love enfolds us and unfolds the petals of truth, goodness, beauty and serenity dormant in our divine core.

Those feet, those lessons, that love are available for seekers everywhere, wherever they are. One step is enough to contact him. He has announced, "I am all over the world, every inch of it." "I do not weigh credentials. If you need me, you deserve me." "Transmute your heart into a Prasanthi Nilayam (The Abode of Supreme Peace); I shall gladly stay therein. Accept me as your sarathi (charioteer), as Arjuna did when I was Krishna; I shall guide you to victory. I shall allay your doubts and fears, teaching you the Gita which you need."

No fear is too formidable for him, no doubt is too desperate. His smile is as sun to the fog. Ask; he answers. Knock; he welcomes. Droop; he makes you bloom. He is the nearest and the readiest refuge. He tells us, "I have no name, nor do I belong to any one place. Call me by any name; I shall respond. Long for me from any place; you can see me there. When you confess, 'I am yours', I reply, 'You are mine'."

When Swami resides in the Prasanthi Nilayam, we prepare for him in our hearts, he blesses us with his counsel on every occasion of need. These messages are his gifts of Grace. They are authentic Sai gold minted into shining coins for furthering happier living and deeper loving.

Swami has revealed that he is neither man nor angel, nor sage nor saint. He is the Teacher of Truth, he says. He teaches us at all times and in all places and through all means. Each message from him to those who plead and pray is a boon to be adored in gratitude.

Brother Lucas Ralli has earned these precious messages, these unique Gita lessons, and won approval to share them with us. The Avatar has come to rescue mankind from disaster. Let us be warned in time; let us listen to the lessons enshrined in this book and surrender our "wills" and "wonts" to his all comprehensive love.

N. KASTURI<br>
Editor, Sanathana Sarathi<br>
Prasanthi Nilayam<br>
India

# INTRODUCTION

In 1979, I picked up a magazine and opened it at random. My eyes fell on an article about Sai Baba and this was my first introduction to our beloved Baba.

For many years I had been searching for the truth and an acceptable philosophy of life and here I found the answer overnight in the teachings of Sri Sathya Sai Baba. I was even more fortunate as I also found that I could link up in meditation with my new master and receive messages from him.

I was so fascinated that I wanted to go to India immediately to see this wonderful holy man. But, one of the earliest messages said quite clearly, "Not now, later." However, in the summer of 1980, I received another message which said, "I will speak to you in Bombay." That seemed more encouraging. The following January I set off for India with three friends and spent three weeks in Bangalore, visiting Brindavan twice a day to see Baba. Our return home via Bombay coincided with a short visit by Baba to that city and, on the very last day, we were granted a private interview at Dharmakshetra in Bombay. Swami duly spoke to us in Bombay, as He had said in the message, and our interview lasted more than half an hour, an unbelievable experience.

In October 1981, we were back again in India and, by this time, I was receiving much longer messages. At a private interview I decided to ask Swami for confirmation that the messages were definitely from Him. His answer was, "Yes, where do you think they come from, the sky?" I also asked if I could share some of these beautiful messages with others and his reply was "You must, you must."

On our latest visit, I asked Swami if I could publish some of the messages in a book so that everyone could share them, and He gave His blessing. It is, therefore, my privilege to offer this book at the lotus feet of our Lord, Bhagavan Baba, and I hope that readers will find these messages as uplifting as I have done in the past.

L.R.

# PART I

# LOVE

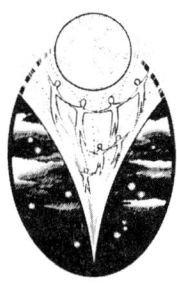

Love is the message for today.

Why do you think I give you messages, day after day, about love? It is because love is God and this is the way to find God and to bring God into your lives.

But few of you listen! You are so embedded in materialism that your minds fail to absorb or grasp the significance of what I am telling you. So I repeat My message, over and over again.

There is no other path to God except through love and service. Love comes first because it leads you on to service, that is service that comes from the heart. This is the only service that is of any value. You serve because of the love that wells up in your heart. It is so strong, this flow of love, My love, that it impels you to share it with others and you can best do this through simple service to humanity, helping the sick, the poor and the suffering. All are My children and all are crying out for love.

Each one of you should be a channel for the outpouring of My love all over the world.

My source of love is unlimited, it fills the whole universe and even then it overflows. How can you turn away and refuse the opportunity which I have given each one of you in this lifetime?

Turn to God, drink in the divine love that I offer you and experience the feeling of divine bliss which will come when you yourself are so full of love that it overflows and reaches all around you.

That is a state of divine bliss and leads to liberation and merging with God.

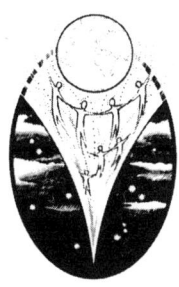

Love is the very basis of the universe. Without love there would be no universe. Love is everywhere. Even the plants experience and express love. Have you not witnessed this? Man is the highest form of nature upon the earth plane but, with most people, the love which they express in their lives is barely equal to the love expressed or shown by animals. Think of the love that a dog can show towards its owner.... love and devotion, too!

You cannot live without love, for life without love is empty and meaningless. But many choose to live that way and imagine they are getting pleasure from such a life. But this is not so. Such a life is completely shallow and selfish.

Life must be full of love. Love must manifest itself in everything you do in life, and that means throughout the day. When I say,

"Start the day with love, spend the day with love,

fill the day with love, end the day with love",

I mean just that. You can repeat these words, but do you really put them into practice? So, My message for you today is just one word, "Love" with a capital L. Love each other. Express love whenever you speak to anyone, whether close friend or otherwise. Love is infectious. As you express love, you are a channel for My love, that very same love through which I created the universe in order to see My love manifesting itself in the world. It is my leela, or God's play. Life is just one constant flow of love.

How can you yourself experience My love? First, by linking up with Me at all moments of the day. But, equally important, by service to your fellow man. There are a thousand forms of service and a thousand ways in which you can be a channel to express My love. It is through this service to your fellow man that you can feel the nourishing effects of My love and allow it to warm the innermost part of your body and soul.

This day I send my special love to each one of you. Treat it like a lighted candle, nourish it, protect it, and pass on the light and the warmth that goes with it to everyone you meet. Truly learn to love one another.

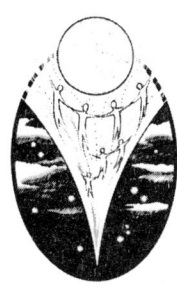

**D**evotion and love flow from the heart, which is the core of your very being. It is the source of all true feeling because it comes from the real you, and the real you is also Me.

When you tune in to your own heart you will feel a vibration of loving warmth which is really emanating from your Mother. I am that Mother. But you seem far away from your Mother because you have created barriers which separate you, barriers which allow you to divert all your attention to worldly and material matters and pleasures.

Fortunately, these barriers can be removed much more easily than the physical barriers which you put up on roads and elsewhere. You yourself have just removed the barrier for a few precious moments while you prepare to receive this message. What you must do is to remove that barrier for ever. At the moment you treat your heart like a sluice gate, lifted up on occasions to let the water through, lowered again to stop the flow.

That flow of water is like My love. Think of it like that and consider whether it would not be better to remove that artificial barrier for ever. Then you would have a permanent flowing in of the love of the Lord and your whole life would change and become more harmonious.

This applies to everyone because very few are really open

to receive My love. The love is there in abundance but I do not force it upon you. You yourselves have the freedom to receive it or shut it out, and the decision is yours alone.

But how do you go about opening it for ever?

Open your hearts, then stop and contemplate the glory of the Lord. Talk to the Lord and turn to Him at every moment of the day. Know that He walks beside you and is always there, just waiting for your call.

He knows everything, sees everything, feels everything, yet wants nothing except your love, for that is the way in which you can be led back to the Kingdom of Heaven. And that is where you will reside, in the heart of the Lord Himself.

Open your hearts, My children, and see the light. Come out of the darkness and leave behind you the illusion which surrounds you and clouds your vision. I am here, I am there, waiting for you NOW.

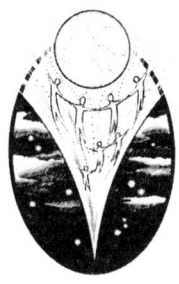

My love is like a mountain towering over each one of you. Do not turn away from that mountain of love, but blend with it at all moments of the day. Love is God and God is love. Love is the certain way to God, so bring God into your lives and forget all your petty problems and quarrels. I am with you now and I know your every thought. Not all your thoughts are good, so watch your thoughts and concentrate on bringing love into your lives. I love you all in spite of your many failings.

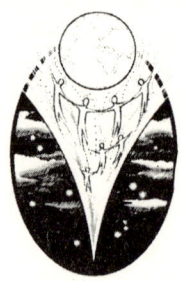

Love flows when you gather together in My name.

Love is the galvanising force in the universe, the very life force itself. And yet, true love is what is missing in so many of your lives.

Why is this? It is simply because you have become lost on the path, drawn away by material pursuits and interests.

The reawakening of man is at hand, reawakening to the certain knowledge that man himself is God. The human body is not you, it simply houses the soul, or the spark of divinity within, for God dwells in the heart of every man and that indwelling spark of the divine is you yourself. All else is illusion! Contemplate that thought and, when the truth unfolds, you will find your true identity; then your whole life pattern will change and you will see everyone in the same light.

At the same time you must find the way to crucify the ego and overcome desire, the two main hinderances to spiritual growth.

My children, all of you are Mine and My love for each one of you is unlimited. When you open your hearts to that love, My divine love will flow and you yourself will rise to the higher levels of consciousness until, one day, you reach the Christ level of consciousness, when you and God really become one.

No one is here today by accident. All of you are on the same path. Each one has the same opportunity to take a great step forward along the spiritual path towards liberation and the final merging with God, the source of your very being.

But you must learn to give up attachment, to forget about self, to conquer the ego, to lose all sense of desire, and then you will have prepared yourself for the future. As you progress, so will the heart open more and more, and love will flow as a perpetual stream from an unlimited source. Your life will then be devoted to helping fellow man, humanity, and only in this way will you find fulfilment and eventual liberation.

Follow the teachings of the Lord and you will find that fulfilment, also peace and tranquillity, and liberation from the material bonds that bind you so firmly to the physical body and the affairs of the earth. Let My love flow through you so that each one of you becomes a beacon of love and light.

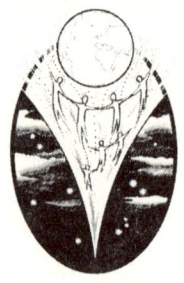

LOVE is the foundation of the whole universe.

God is love, and love is the only route that leads to God. How can anyone doubt this? But if it is so, and it is so, why is it that so many people, devotees and others, fail to bring love into their lives?

The reasons are clear: separation. These people are lost on the path and they have even lost their identity. Who are you? Just think about it for a few moments and tell Me what you think. Do you really believe what you are telling Me? If so, then remember what you have said and from now on lead your life and behave in a way that reflects that knowledge, the certainty that you yourself are God, and that God is love.

> Never again an angry word.
> Never again an evil thought.
> Never again an evil act.

Replace all these evils with love, My love, and then all evil will be eradicated and the world will become a happier place. Man has virtually destroyed the world through evil thought, selfishness, greed and jealousy. But all is not lost and all can be saved. A new age dawns and the Divine Avatar is here in your very midst. How lucky you are to be here at the same time as He. Do you realise that? But, once again, what are you doing about it? Words and incantations are not enough.

Action is required, action to cleanse the world. Love is the cleansing medicine. So go out into the world and fill the world with love. I will help you, I will guide you but, in the end, it is up to you, whether you listen to My words and take some positive action, or continue with the same bad habits that have led so many of you to the very edge of the precipice of destruction. It is never too late to change.

Think about it and make a new start today.

God is love, love is God; truly, there is only God. Everything else is illusion and transitory. Do not continue chasing shadows.

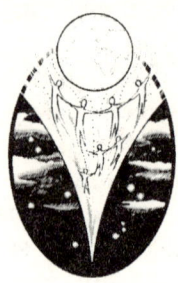

Love leads to unity and a realisation of the truth that all are one.

Love is the motivating force in the universe, for love is God.

Approach everyone and everything with love and then the frustrations of the past will evaporate.

See love manifesting all around you, in the flowers, the trees, every part of nature, all part of God.

It is when love is blocked that you separate yourself from the Lord, and then you live on another (material) plane, where even pleasure and happiness are forms of illusion, for such pleasures can never last.

When you fill your life with love, you become permanently attuned to the Lord, and then you experience that divine love which brings with it the peace that passeth all understanding.

Always look on the bright side of everything. Never dwell on the problems or the difficulties that come into your life, since they are simply transient, just like the problems and difficulties of the past. They are little experiences which you need to propel you along the spiritual path and you have brought them into your life for your own good.

My child, unity *is* divinity.

Look for and see that unity in everyone and everything.

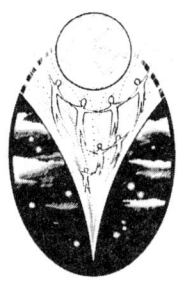

Unity and love are interchangeable. Where there is love, there will be unity; where there is unity, love will flow.

It is My love that flows everywhere in the universe and it is man on earth who disrupts the flow, diverts it, allowing My love to pass him by, leaving him untouched.

As you look around, you can see those who have been touched, for they absorb My love and, at the same time, reflect it, so that My love flows even more freely all around them. But there are too many who are so preoccupied with themselves and their own importance that they miss the unique opportunity which I give them, the opportunity to experience their own divinity.

Remember those words... "I am you, you are Me, all One, all God"... this is what I told you (at the interview) because it is the hallmark of unity. When man realises that he is divine and that all around him is also divine, how can he consider himself so much more important than his neighbour, his friend or his enemy?

My child, you are Mine, and those who hear these words are also My children, all Mine, all a manifestation of My divine love.

Try to instil this knowledge into everyone, an understanding of the true meaning of love, and then all their lives will become so much more happy and fulfilling.

Be like the beacon in the sky, radiating love and light. Imagine a thousand such beacons in the sky, just like the twinkling stars in the distant galaxies that you can see on a clear night. You have the same power within to radiate love and light and you should shine forth like a star from the moment of awakening in the morning until the moment comes for sleep at night.

If you really do this, your whole body and mind will be cleansed because it is My love which is vibrating within you and its power is unlimited.

Sing and laugh and enjoy life. Put behind you all worry and fear, all doubts of any kind.

Know that I am God, you are God, there is only God, all one, complete unity, pure love, pure divinity.

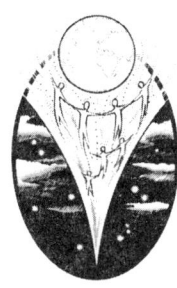

My love surrounds you, encompasses you, has actually created you and you are My love. Where is your love?

Your love can only be a reflection of My love and, when that love fails to flow freely, it is only because you fail to reflect it.

You are the mirror, an image of God, but you have allowed the mirror to become clouded and the love and light can no longer be reflected clearly.

You must look within and find a way to cleanse that mirror; to cleanse the soul by eliminating all the negative aspects, especially the ego, anger, jealousy, greed, desire, ambition and undue concern with material matters.

Turn instead to God, know God, re-establish your divine relationship with God and then, slowly, the mirror will be cleaned and you will be able to experience and reflect My love. A new light will shine from within and bring with it a sense of contentment and happiness which few of you have really experienced.

Love is God and the two will always manifest themselves together.

Be happy, be carefree, be content and know that whatever problems you may have at any time are purely transient and of no permanent consequence.

The Lord waits patiently and observes the progress of man on the spiritual path. You too should watch your progress and realise that you alone can bring about the changes in your life that will lead you back to God, along the only path that will lead there, the spiritual path.

Start the cleansing process today and put aside all negative elements that delay your progress or divert you from the true path.

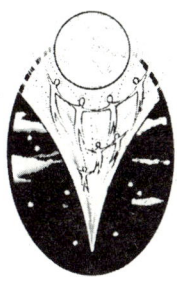

On this lovely early morning, all is quiet, all is peaceful, but where is the love?

Love is in the heart, sometimes locked away, like precious jewellery in the home, but what is the use of having something locked away? Jewellery has no lasting value because when your earth life is over, you cannot take it with you and it is lost to you for ever.

What about love? Love is there always, like the flower in the bud, hidden from sight but, at the right moment, the flower emerges from the bud and brightens all around.

Love is the same, except that you can unlock the love within your heart at will and allow it to change your whole life.

Life without love is empty. Life with love is heaven.

Open your hearts today and let the love, My love, emerge from its resting place and brighten the world around you.

Love is effervescent, full of energy, the very God force itself. That is love in its purest form, the real jewel that can be left on permanent display and never again locked away. But you have to release it, for you alone have the key to your own heart.

This is God's gift to man, His own love that He has poured out in such abundance that it fills the whole universe. How can any of you turn away from that love and continue on the blind narrow path that so many of you follow? You are like cars trying to travel at night, in the darkness, without any light to guide you. How can you make any progress when you can hardly see the road?

Open the heart, switch on the lights and illuminate the path ahead, as well as the whole world around you. Then you will find the way to the kingdom of heaven which is there now, even in this passing moment.

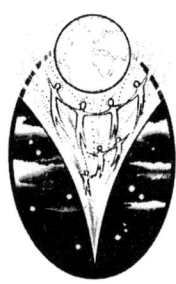

Talk to them [at the meeting] about love, love that fills the universe, love that is effervescent, like the sparkling waves of the ocean.

How can you live without becoming immersed in that mountain of love? Yet, some of you live such shallow lives that you do not even experience My love; you are so preoccupied with material pursuits.

Just pause at this moment in your life and consider where you are going. Have you been blown into a sidewater where you move around in small circles and never really get anywhere?

Some of you are lost on the path, completely immersed in materialism and unable even to see the light that is shining all around you. Look up into the heavens and see that light. Allow it to permeate every corner of your being, to light up your heart and soul, so that you too can be like a lantern, beaming out a great light of love to all around you.

Love is the very basis of the universe. Bring love into your lives and live in total harmony with the Creator who loves you all so much.

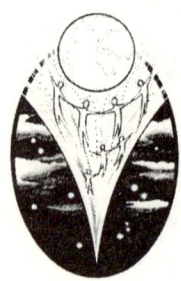

Why do you worry so much? Life should be all happiness and joy! You take everything so seriously; it is not necessary, or good.

Talk about LOVE [at the meeting], for love is the very basis of life. Without love there would be no life.

Try to instil this love, which is My love, into the hearts of everyone. My love is everywhere, wanting and waiting to manifest itself, but man is so busy, too occupied with material pursuits. Love hardly finds a place in his life.

Sow the seeds of love in the hearts of men. Let them feel it, let them experience it, and when they experience My all embracing love, how can they want anything else? All desire falls away. This is the quickest and most certain way to reach the state of desirelessness.

Out of love comes service. Call it seva or any other name, but service is what it means, service to fellow man. And it must be done out of love, not just because you are told to do it by someone else, whether it be the Council, your parents, or any other authority.

Service is the inevitable result of pure love, the very feeling welling up inside you that you must express this love and light up the hearts of all around you. See it like a lighted candle. You yourself have seen this spectacle in Greece at Easter time and will never forget it: the sight of those thousands of flickering candles coming down the hillside in the night from the little church at the top of the hill. All those lights come from the one source, a single candle within the church, and that represents My love, the very source of life and the universe.

So go out into the world and spread My message and My love. Let it reach every corner of the earth, then all darkness will be removed and the evil forces will be overcome. Only love will remain and that is GOD.

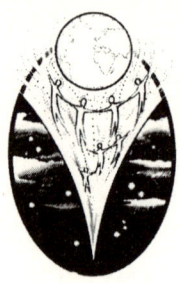

There is calm, there is peace but, without love, there is nothing. When the heart opens, like the lotus, the whole world changes and you can manifest yourself as part of the whole, in perfect harmony with nature and the God force. But, without love you are like a speck of dust, bobbing about on the surface of the ocean, being buffeted by every movement all around you. That is what is happening to so many of you now: there is no love and you are separated from the source, hence you are suffering from the tribulations of all those around you and all the little problems of life.

This type of life cannot be satisfactory and few of you are really happy, even though you try to give that impression.

Awaken, My children, awaken, let love flow into your lives. Love comes from the expanding heart. Open up and let that love, My love, pour out from the centre of your very being. Only then will you experience true happiness and become immune to the worries of the world.

Love is the secret of life for love is God, the only source of true happiness. Open your hearts today and experience the divine bliss which I have given to each one of you.

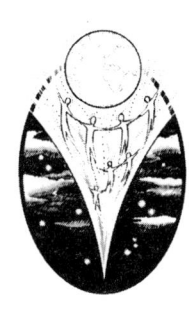

When love flows from the heart, there is such compassion that you develop an overwhelming desire to go out and serve fellow man. It comes from the realisation that all are one, all are part of the whole, and the whole is God.

In reality, you and God are one, and when love flows and you are full of compassion, then you see God in everyone. This is the meaning of unity.

When you serve fellow man you are serving God, for that man is God. What nobler cause could there be?

It is through service that you can become awakened and discover your own reality. Go out into the world and serve fellow man and that will lead to your own salvation.

Let love be the motivating force at all times.

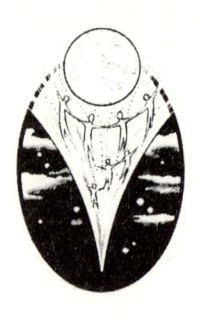

When you gather together in My name, you provide a setting where My love can flow so freely that you may even be overwhelmed by the strength of that love and the feeling of compassion which accompanies it. It breaks down all barriers and reveals the God within, the real you which is God Himself.

I am there always but you do not realise it. It is only when you yourselves create the right conditions that you can experience My omnipresence.

The Sai Groups which have been formed are a starting point and will grow. They must be based on LOVE, devotion and service. Bear this in mind in all that you do and plan. People will be drawn to you when they are ready and I will guide others towards you. Accept them all as children of God, for they are all Mine. Each one of you plays a part in My mission.

When you surrender to the God within, your life will change and you will begin to experience that peace of mind which is normally so elusive. And when you experience that peace, regardless of the conditions around you, then you will know that your life is manifesting itself at the highest level of consciousness, where you and God are one. That is the goal and you will only achieve it through love, for love is God and God is love.

I send My love to all of you, and My blessings.

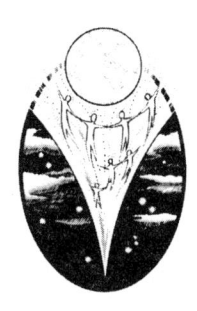

**S**wami's life is Swami's message.

Swami's life is one constant outpouring of LOVE, for love is the life force itself and I am the source of that love.

Love is infectious once it is allowed to flow. That is the secret of happiness, to open your hearts and let the love flow. Let it flow everywhere, to every corner of your own being, all around you, to friends and enemies alike, to the animals, to the plants and trees, then further afield, to other areas and other countries so that love fills the earth plane as indeed it fills the whole universe.

What prevents the flow of love? The answer is, all the negative aspects, starting with the ego itself which is man's biggest problem. No real progress can be made on the spiritual path while man allows his ego to remain in the ascendant. Ego, attachment, desire, anger, frustration, greed, all these are the enemy and must be overcome. Meditation on truth is the way, for in moments of divine peace, you can find your true self and become attuned to the Godhead (or the Atma). But desire and attachment hold man back, and he becomes obsessed with material matters, failing to realise that all these are a form of illusion, here today, gone tomorrow. Man places false values on so many worldly things, possessions and wealth being the main ones. Man too becomes obsessed with worldly power and position. But what are these in the eyes of God? They are transitory and will lead you nowhere.

Man must break away from all this and look for salvation elsewhere. Eventually, he turns to God and starts that long spiritual journey which ultimately leads him to salvation and liberation.

To live My message means to live in love, to see God in everyone and everything, to treat everyone as though they are God. Could anything be simpler? Learn to radiate love so that it affects all around you. See the transforming effect which it has, even on flowers and plants. Be like a beacon in the sky, radiating love and light. That is my message for all of you. I am the source of that love and light, never doubt that, or the power of the divine Avatar.

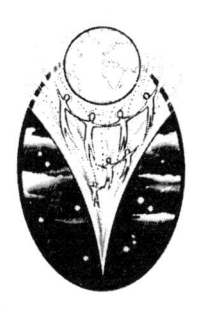

I am LOVE, the very embodiment of love.

When love flows from your heart, the very words of the Lord pour out, and these are worth a thousand times anything that man can conceive with his limited brain.

Life is eternity. Tomorrow is a point in eternity, as you see it, and you identify that moment of time. But I do not identify any moment of time for all is NOW, the past, the present and the future. Yes, all is NOW for Me as I have willed it that way.

I play out what seems to be a never ending game, perhaps God's game, but it is divine. One day you will marvel at the beauty of the permanent leela that is the work of the Lord.

I will always love you for you are My children. You must learn to love Me too for that is the only path that will lead you back to Me and enable you to realise your own divinity.

Have faith, have love, have compassion; serve, love and help your fellow man, that is the path to divinity.

The three year birthday programme, what is that? It is just another path to lead man towards Me and the divine state. But I have no birthday.

You are thinking of bodies, but I have always been. Only My body changes and it changes at will, according to the need of the times. I have had a million "births", in this form and that, even now I stand beside you in yet another form. You may not see Me but some may feel My presence.

LOVE, LOVE, LOVE, I am here because of My love for each one of you, My jewels, that is how I see you.

Try to see Me as the only jewel that you could ever desire, and then you will eventually achieve divinity.

# PART II

# OTHER THEMES

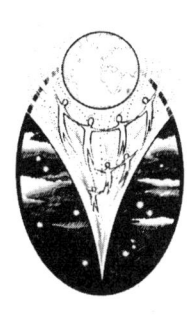

## LIFE WITHOUT LOVE

I am with you always, even though you do not see Me. Where am I? In the very heart of each one of you. So you can feel Me, experience Me, feel My love and compassion even though you may not see Me.

Why do you not love one another? How is it possible that there are these jealousies, even in the Sai movement? They are there because man is full of ego, and he will not learn to control his sensual feelings and his desires for, and love of, material things and material satisfaction. How misguided is such a man. What is his real reward? Just for a short while he imagines that he has achieved something and he experiences some form of pleasure and satisfaction. But these feelings are temporary and cannot last. However, he who worships the Lord, loves the Lord, and loves and serves his fellow man, he will find a lasting reward, that is, an inner peace which leads him to nirvana.

So drop these stupid habits and attachments. Wake up and see how hollow is the life that some of you are leading. For life without love and life without God is totally empty and unfulfilling.

Make the decision today to do something about it. It is

never too late to start unless you never start. Have *you* started? If not, start today, in the presence of the Lord.

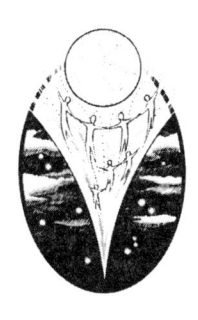

## FREEDOM

Liberty is freedom of the mind, freedom of action in all that you do. You have your laws in every country and you are required to live within the framework of those laws, but this still leaves you with great freedom in the way that you actually live and behave.

Examine this freedom and the way that you live, and consider whether you are also living your life according to the laws of God. What are those laws? They are reflected in the teachings of the Lord, teachings which have been handed down over many centuries, teachings which have been reinforced by the divine incarnation of the Sai Avatar. Notice the similarity in the teachings of Christ and the Prophets and the teachings which I offer to you today.

God is Love. Bring love into your lives and you will approach the Kingdom of Heaven, not a place, as you understand it, but a state of being, a level of consciousness, the Christ level of consciousness where you and God unite and become one.

This is the goal of every living soul and it is a path which may seem long and arduous, but that is only because so few of you tread the path in the right way, or even in the right direction.

You need a compass, a Sai compass, that is a compass which reflects the teachings of Sai. If you steer your way forward with the Sai compass, you will reach the goal and you will experience on the path showers of Sai love which fall on you from all directions. That is the food which you need to sustain you on the journey, and it is the only food which will give you the sustenance which your body and soul require on the long journey.

Start that journey afresh today, equipped with the Sai compass and never waver from the path, regardless of the distractions which you experience during the journey.

Desire will remain until love fills your heart to such an extent that there is no longer room for anything else. When love overflows, as it does when the Lord showers it upon you, then and only then do you become immune to any aspect of earthly desire. At that stage you see only God, desire only God, and finally you become God with the complete merging of the soul.

That is ultimate liberation and everyone's goal.

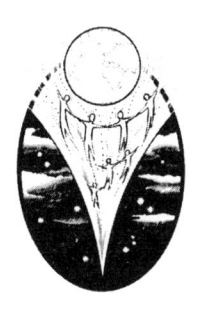

## NEGATIVE FEELINGS

Purity, harmony, unity, divinity, love, co-operation, service, all these are positive.

Ego, jealousy, anger, desire, all these are negative.

Each group represents the opposites.

When you experience any of the negative feelings, just look for the opposite. It is like a coin. Toss the coin and it turns up tails. Turn it over and you get heads.

Everyday you will experience some of the negative feelings, frustration being one of them, and it arises from the negative elements which I have mentioned.

As soon as these negative feelings become apparent, replace them immediately with thoughts of love, harmony, unity, divinity, and a feeling that all is one, all is God. Then your negative feelings will be dissipated and replaced with something positive.

It is a form of mental exercise and you can practise it throughout the day.

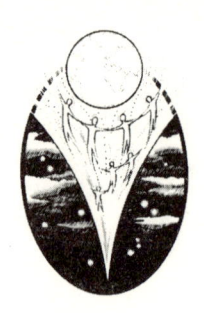

## SECURITY AND INSECURITY

Uncertainty is familiar to all of you. You know the past, you think you know the present, but the future is known only to God. Why is that?

If you knew everything, you would stagnate and there would be no incentive to act. But it is only through activity, soul activity, that you can find your way back to God. Uncertainty is therefore a necessity of life and it should make you look inside, look outside, and look all around you so that you can assess the situation. You then become curious and wonder what is going to happen, perhaps this or that...?

But the plan of God is certain, it is known, it is timeless, everyone is involved and you are all part of that plan. God's plan is the plan of the universe and encompasses everything within, from the most distant galaxies to the smallest living matter on earth.

You should think about this and consider how you relate to the whole. Your future is known to God and He knows that all will eventually find the true path. But due to the timeless nature of God's creation, and the free will which God has given to man, you retain the freedom to decide when to take positive action to move along the path. You can delay for one life and the next and lives beyond that, and many of you will do this. But once you are awakened to the truth, you should take that action now, action which you know must be taken sooner or later. Why delay? You delay because you are so immersed in material pursuits that you do not want to change. You feel the present way of life offers security, convenience and some happiness, but is that really so? If so, you are leading a life of illusion.

What should you do? What *would* you do if you really believed the truth? Would you not do something? Would you not make some changes in your life style and the way you behave, especially towards other people?

Once you become aware of the omnipresence of God, how can you ignore Him and leave Him out of your life to the extent that you now do? Most of you are oblivious to the fact that you and God are one and that you yourself are part of the whole, which itself is God. So bring God into your daily lives, talk to Him and have a continuous dialogue with Him during the day, and let it be His will in all that you do. Surrender to that will and know that He will take care of you. Then and then only will peace come into your life; and all the worries of the past and the present will be seen to be what they really are, a manifestation of separation from God and a failure to surrender to His will. It is your will that has been in the ascendant during the past and your will has not produced the peace of mind which you would like to enjoy. Peace of mind can only come after surrender. From that point on it is impossible to experience fear, anxiety, insecurity, worry or the lack of anything, for God will provide for all your needs.

That is the state of bliss, the point at which you approach the threshold of the total merging of the soul with the Lord Himself.

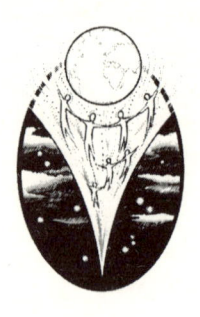

## FACING UP
## TO LIFE'S DIFFICULTIES

It is good that you ask Me, for you are confused, and even though all is God, confusion can and does exist.

The manifestation of God is at many levels because all levels are simply different aspects of God. God is everyone and everything. So, when you consider the problems that face you, contemplate the thought that all is God, even all problems are God, just different manifestations.

You have to decide how to relate to all this and the particular experiences that come to you in each life time. Sudden decisions to do this or that, or to opt out of this or that, will only bring what appears to be temporary relief, a token satisfaction. But the fact that these experiences have come to you in this life is the important thing, because it means you have a direct opportunity to face such problems, solve them, learn from the lessons which they bring, and then pass on, leaving behind a cleaner slate. If, however, you shy away, you merely postpone the working out of this part of your karmic state. So, be like the wise souls who welcome difficulties and grasp the chance to face them and, thus, the opportunity to move ahead on the spiritual path.

Look at all problems in this way, as opportunities, not real difficulties. At the same time, you get the opportunity to help others whose past karmas are inextricably linked to your own.

Everything will fall into place, although seldom in quite the way you expect, but that is not important. What is important is that you remain intact, on the path, and do not allow yourself to be drawn away to some sidewater, where you appear to find rest, but which takes you away from the true spiritual path. Contemplate all these thoughts as you decide what to do.

It is right to be firm, but fair, when you are in a position of trust and authority. Do not lower yourself to the levels which some people reach in moments of anger, because that will not do anyone any good, nor will it solve the problem.

Be kind, be understanding, be tolerant, be logical, be true to your own self and do not be influenced by emotion, whether it is your own or the emotion of others around you.

I will help you. The problems are not as big as you think. There is nothing which cannot be solved with a little patience, love and understanding.

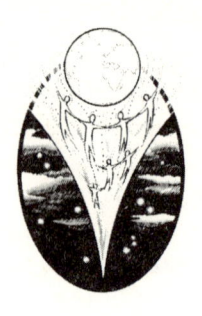

## OBSTACLES

**M**y children, you have changed already and the process continues and will continue. In a little while you will move into calmer waters and you will benefit (within) from the experiences which you have been through. Really, you should welcome these obstacles, which present you with the chance to wipe the slate clean in this lifetime. Believe Me, what I tell you is the truth, and you should meditate upon My words so that you do not let this chance slip by. That would be the tragedy, not what is happening, for that is really here for your own good. If you look dispassionately at what is going on, it is life working itself out. You, like Me, are the witnesses. How do I react? I sit, I watch, I help, but seldom do I interfere. You should do much the same, except that you should always concentrate on giving whatever help you can to those around you, those souls who come into your lives for one reason or another.

It is never as bad as you think at the time. Look at the traumas of the past and how they are now all in the past. Is that not so? Soon the traumas of today will also be in the past; and all that matters is what you have learnt from the experiences. So, welcome the obstacles and never fear them.

    Live in truth, then nothing can touch or harm you, for you are God Himself and God is untouchable.

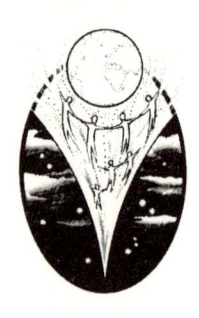

## VIOLENCE IN THE WORLD

All is in the balance all the time. Everything works itself out according to the past and everything that happens now is the result of the past. Recent events are no exception.

Only the Lord can see the past, the total past of everyone and everything, every event and even every thought. Only the Lord can see the future, as He can see that picture now, the creation of the past, the present and the future, all are NOW to Him. But the picture changes as man progresses on the spiritual path, and you should never despair even when you witness some tragic event like the recent violence.

What should you think at such a time? You should concentrate on your own personal sadhana. Examine yourself and your own progress on the spiritual path. Are you changing as time passes? Have you given up those bad habits of the past? Are you full of love, like a fountain which continually throws out its water in a beautiful cascade? You should emulate the fountain and become a fountain of love, Sai love. For it is love alone that can save man and the earth itself from destruction.

Love is God and, when it flows freely, it means that you are allowing God to enter into your life.

See the world as it is, a training ground. Do not waste the opportunity to get that training, so that you are better prepared for the next stage in your evolution. God provides the facilities, God shows you how to use them, but you have to take the initiative and make your own decisions.

Be positive in all your thoughts and, when disaster strikes, realise that it is simply a passing phase, something to overcome. Such is the event to which you refer. In a hundred years it will be in the history books and, at that time, those souls who are here on earth will be worrying about other matters.

So, look ahead, not backwards, and know that the divine awakening lies ahead. The path is through God, with God, in God, always remembering that God is Love.

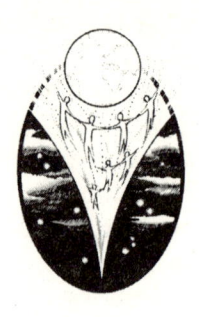

## DEPRESSION

Depression is isolation, that is, separation from God. How could a man, filled with the love of God, aware of God's presence twenty-four hours a day, living his life in harmony with God, ever get depressed?

Depression results from ignorance and the lack of awakening or any desire to find the truth or to find God Himself.

Such people can be helped through others who can enlighten them. The truth has no bounds, for the truth is an aspect of God and represents the whole.

It is this isolation from God that is man's greatest problem and it results from years of separation, during which man has chosen to reside in the wilderness instead of the heaven that lies within his own being.

Life with God is bliss. Life without God is depressing and totally unsatisfying and unfulfilling.

Go out into the world and spread the message of the Lord. Let My message spread to every corner of the earth. In the end the truth will prevail and peace and harmony will return to the world.

It will take time, for man has free will and God will not

take away the gift that He has given to mankind, a gift which is balanced by the love which the Lord pours out and showers upon you, regardless of the state of your soul.

You have love, you have freedom, you have everything and you alone can make the choice of which path to follow. It is like a maze: some confusion, false starts, sudden dead ends and then new beginnings. But all the time there is only one path that leads out of the maze, the path back to God. Everyone will find it in the end but, for some, it may take aeons of time before they see the light, that is, the light which is always there to guide them along the right path.

Man is distracted by desire and by the apparent fascination of material things, all of them a form of illusion. Look around you now and consider what is the truth and what is transient. How much of what you see will be there and in that form for ever? How can these things, these attractions, give you satisfaction for ever? They are transient, illusion, here today and gone tomorrow.

Do not get immersed in material things or be overcome by desire. These will weigh you down and divert you from the only path that is worth following. Yes, My children, you are in a maze and you must find your way out. Resolve to leave the maze and know that, when you do get out, you will find salvation and eternal bliss which lie at the end of the road. This is where the Lord Himself waits for you and, when you arrive, He will take you into His arms and you will merge with Him for ever more.

## FOOD FOR THE LORD

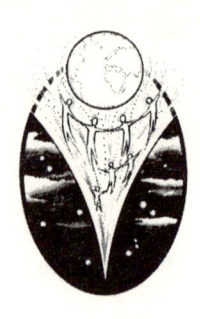

Food for the Lord is a manifestation of your utter devotion and love of the Lord. It must come from your heart, not from your kitchen. I am hungry, but only for your love.

You are so immersed in life on earth, in all its aspects, some pleasant, some not so pleasant and you associate yourself with those aspects. Turn to the higher self, the real you within, and then slowly the higher self will begin to manifest and your life will change, your whole outlook will change because, when this happens, you are bound to be happy. It is the beginning of the path to ultimate and permanent bliss. Association with life on the material plane can never bring permanent relief for the needs of the soul. It is merely a playground for the desires of the lower aspects of man: the body, mind and senses. There is desire, there is mind, but there is no way to satisfy the unquenchable thirst of the mind and all its many desires. You can have this or that, but it simply leads to more desires, and then even more.

But free will always exists in man. While you are ignorant about spiritual matters, there is no choice. However, as you become awakened, the knowledge comes to the surface and you are presented with a challenge. You are in that position now. It can last over many lifetimes, until you make the only choice that can resolve the dilemma and lead you out of the darkness towards the light. All physical experience is an aspect of darkness, or the unreal. It is like a temporary fog which covers the ground and obscures the beautiful view that actually lies in front of you. You are the creator of that fog and only you can clear it away.

Think about these things and know that the solution to your problems lies in releasing that power house of love that is stored within. When you open the gates and allow that love, My love, to pour out and manifest itself all around you, then the fog will clear and you will see the way ahead. When that happens you will be offering Me the food for which I am patiently waiting.

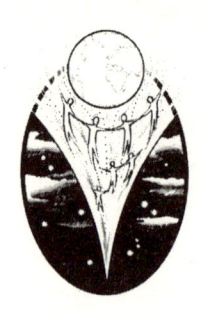

## FREE WILL

You have free will and you exercise it every minute of the day. Are you not aware of this? But Swami is the controller of the universe and plans the pattern of events far into the future. You are all involved in that plan, however big or small is the part that you are to play in Swami's plans. You can interfere with Swami's plans, and man has done so, but the eventual outcome of Swami's plans is always inevitable according to Swami's will. You may delay an event or cause it to happen in a slightly different way to the way Swami would wish, but Swami is the great balancer and will always restore the balance within the world whenever He wishes.

So do not think you do not have free will. You do and it is right that you exercise it every minute of the day. As you evolve, you will use that free will in the correct way and link it perfectly to Swami's plans, for all Swami's plans are perfect. Sometimes you will make mistakes but that does not matter, so long as you learn from them.

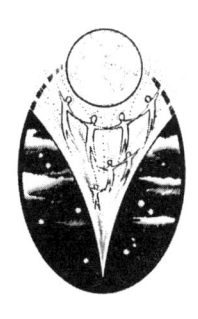

## UNITY (I)

I am the Lord of the universe and I control the elements. But I have created man with free will.

Man must learn to work, not only for God but also for fellow man. If you devote your lives to such a commitment, then you will find true peace, happiness and fulfilment. But if you seek your own personal pleasure and satisfaction through material things, then you will be sorely disappointed and end up getting nowhere. It is the same with the search for status and power. Which power seeker ever reached a state of bliss or found the way back to the Godhead?

So, remember these things. Be leaders and help others, but remain humble at all times. You cannot lead anyone effectively if your position as leader means anything to you other than the chance to serve fellow man. Otherwise your attention will be diverted into the wrong channels.

Above all things, learn to work as a team for that is what you are, and then the concept of individual leaders will be overcome. You are the Atma, so is fellow man, so is everything, so where are the leaders? The Atma has no leaders; there are only those who draw closer to God and travel in the right direction on the spiritual path.

The future of the young people in England is vital to the future of that country. You have the chance to improve that future if you choose to follow My teachings. Unite in service and dedicate your lives to working for humanity. I will help you. I am with you now, even as I speak these words. I will watch over you. I will be with you every moment of every day so I will always know your thoughts and observe your actions.

Remember this and try to please Me, knowing that you have been chosen for a vital task to be carried out in the name of the Lord.

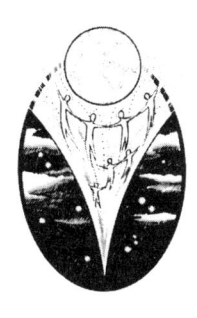

## GOD AND RELIGION

Every religion looks for God and they look far and wide, but man should know that God is omnipresent and resides in the very heart of man.

Truly, there is only one religion, the religion of love, but on earth there are many religions, all of which lead along the same path to the ultimate, omnipresent God.

Call God by any name for all names belong to God. Pray to God in any form and your prayers will reach the omnipresent God, provided only that the prayer comes from the heart.

God is the eternal witness and you are the children of that living God. He is here, He is there, He is everywhere, for God is omnipresent, always has been and always will be.

The path of the soul is long and arduous, for man has lost his way and forgotten his real identity and his relationship with God. But man himself is divine, a spark of the omnipresent God and it is through the kindling of that spark that man can become re-awakened to the truth and his own divinity within, the true nature of his being.

Man is part of the whole and that whole is God. In truth, all is God, simply different manifestations.

Now is the time of great awakening and an opportunity for man to know himself and to re-establish his true relationship with God.

Every religion teaches you to love one another and you should remember that love is the greatest force in the universe. God is love in its highest form and man should strive to let that love manifest itself in his own life at all times. Love ye one another and recognise the God dwelling in the heart of every living being. When man recognises the omnipresent God in everyone, friend and foe, only then will peace return to earth. The time of awakening is now and all thoughts of differences must be put behind you.

They say that all roads lead to Rome, but it is better to say that all roads lead to God. Every religion is a different pathway to the same destination.

All religions are really one and love is the motivating force behind all of them. Love is God, and God is love. Learn to love one another, then you will find an inner peace which will spread to others and help to bring peace and happiness to this troubled world.

Know at all times that God is there, watching over you and aware of every thought that passes through your mind. Meditate on that thought and try to improve your life by living in perfect harmony with God, the God that dwells in your own heart as the silent witness.

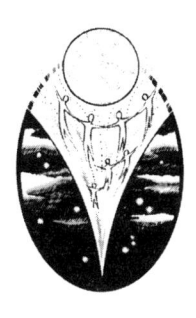

## MAN'S IDENTITY

Within man is all knowledge, past, present and future, but it is at levels of consciousness which are lost to man unless he is manifesting at the highest levels. At the highest level, man and God are one. All are God in truth, but the God aspect only manifests itself to the extent that man rises up to those levels. All levels are there, always have been, for God created man in His own image.

You cannot and never will understand the origin of man for God alone knows and understands how man was created. Therefore, just live with the certain knowledge that all are God, all are one, all part of the whole. Only when you understand this, that there is only God, can you begin to understand the truth about life.

But is is so, always has been and always will be. The fact that it does not appear to be so is simply illusion, illusion created by man himself. It is the choice of man to tread that path for man has been given free will.

Life is a game but its end is inevitable. God could bring the game to an end at any moment, just like picking up a pack of cards when the game goes wrong, putting all the cards back in the pack where they came from and starting again, another game.

Do not be worried by the mystery of life. Far more important is to live the life while you have it and spread the knowledge to those who can benefit from it.

I will always be with you and I continue to shower My love upon all of you, all My children.

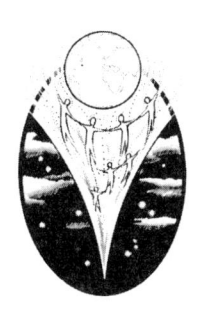

## SPIRITUAL EFFORT (I)

I am the Alpha and the Omega, the beginning and the end, and everything that happens is known to Me for I have willed the very creation of the universe.

The matters which concern man and occupy his mind are normally so trivial and he wastes much of his life worrying about them. In fact, they are unimportant and of no lasting consequence.

Start at the beginning... Who are you? When you know the answer to that question, that you yourself are God, then surely you will change your life style and the way you behave.

God is LOVE, and yet true love is absent in so many of your lives. How can there be all these stupid petty jealousies, even within the Sai organisation? What have you learned by becoming devotees? How many of you are progressing spiritually? Do you realise I am here always, watching every movement, every thought of each one of you?

Is that not a challenge? It should be! You all have this supreme opportunity which I have given you, and yet many will fritter away the chance to find salvation and eventual liberation.

Effort is required, effort motivated by love. Where is the love? Bring love into your lives and learn the secret that inner peace can only be found if and when you manifest yourself at the higher levels.

How do you start? Start with love. Fill the day with love. Let the love fill your whole being so that you radiate love like a giant beacon in the sky.

Stop and think. Contemplate yourself and your life pattern. That is a good starting point.

Stop and think who you are, what you are doing in this life. Is it all good, does it please and satisfy you? Or, more important, does it please God, the real you that is part of God?

Examine yourselves and make a real effort to start again, this time on the right lines, Sai lines, and live a life so full of love that all negative thoughts are eliminated from your mind for ever more.

I give My love and blessings to all of you.

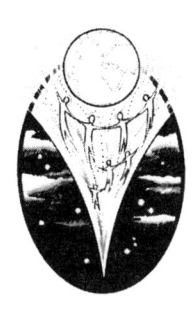

## THE SAI MISSION

Why does the Lord incarnate at this time? It is to save the world from destruction by man himself.

Man has sunk to the lowest levels in his craving for power and material pursuits and he has become obsessed with himself. He has forgotten his true spiritual nature and his own true identity. So the Lord incarnates at such a time to lead man back along the forgotten path and to guide him onto it, the spiritual path. It is not easy and it takes time but that is the Sai mission.

How is it achieved? By education and re-education, hence the very big educational projects in India with special schools, colleges, and now the University. These are the seeds which the Lord is sowing and they will produce results all over the world. The beginning may seem slow, but later, the pace will quicken and nothing will be able to stand in the way or obstruct the will of the Lord.

You are all involved in this mission and you have a great opportunity and responsibility. Do not let that chance slip by you, for it may never come again. Listen to My words and try to respond in a way which will bring happiness into your own life and into the lives of many others.

*Swami, what about Sai activities?*

Activity is ACTION, Sai action, and that means selfless service to humanity. You must work, you must serve, you must forget self. Be happy to sacrifice yourself for the benefit of others.

Love is the motivating force, divine love, for that is the seed which I have planted in each one of you. Let the seed grow, let the love flow, let the love, My love, heal the hearts of men and save the world from death and destruction. It is only through love and understanding that the world can be saved and you, all of you, are My instruments.

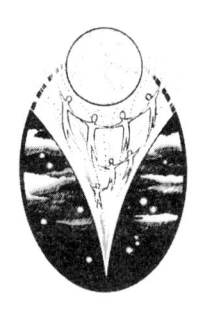

## THE INNER VOICE

I come out of nowhere to speak to you because I am everywhere, always with you. So I am always communicating with those who are open and ready to receive My messages. My teachings are clear and have been repeated so many times in a language that all can understand.

Most of you here today [at the meeting] have been to see Me in India. Many will come again. Some of you I will call especially because you can play an important part in spreading My message, and thus help others to see the light that shines throughout the universe. You yourselves are part of that light but few of you know it. Do you remember My words, "BE LIKE A BEACON IN THE SKY, RADIATING LOVE AND LIGHT, THAT IS WHAT YOU CAN DO FOR SWAMI"? Love and light are everywhere, but many people still choose to live in darkness, and they keep the shutters securely closed while they concentrate on enjoying, as they imagine, the material and sensual pleasures of life on earth. But how can any of you here today ever close those shutters again, once you have seen and experienced the crystal clear light shining through even the smallest crack? You must always move towards the light, for I am that light and the ultimate goal is to merge with Me in a pool of light and experience pure bliss. That is nirvana and it is a state of bliss which is beyond the comprehension of the human mind.

You have to live on earth for a while, and you see Me, too, living also on earth these days. I appear to live just like a man but I am only here and in this human form for your benefit. So do not lose the opportunity to learn from Me while I am here. You are lucky, indeed, that you have incarnated at this time and it is not by accident that this has happened. So, if you have found Me, do not throw away the chance which you now have to move far along the path.

Now, about communication, all can communicate with Me and all should try. Special gifts come to those who have earned them, but all of you have some gift. Silence is the beginning in the art of communication. Learn to live in silence for some moments every day. Just sit in complete silence and listen for the voice of God. You may not physically hear a voice because God can speak to you through the silence, and you will become aware of God's message, even though you hear no voice. Is this not the way in which you yourself receive the messages? So, let your mind rest on Me in those moments of silence and then the thoughts will come into your mind. But, be patient and do not necessarily expect immediate results. Success will come provided you persevere.

Know always that I am with you, even when you hear nothing. For I am you and you are Me, so how is it possible that we cannot communicate? Just think about these things and do not give up easily or allow anyone or anything to divert you from the path that will lead you to nirvana.

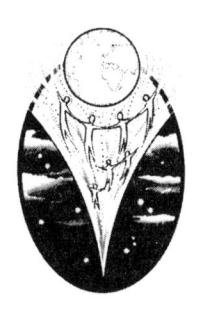

## SURRENDER (I)

Every day there is a message, a message to uplift the heart, to raise all of you to the higher levels of consciousness. This is the spiritual path, upwards to the higher levels until you reach the divine level where you and God are one. It may seem very remote, even though that divine level of consciousness is within you now. It is only a question of the level at which you choose to express your life.

When you surrender totally to the Lord and forget about self, then you are preparing the way. While you concern yourself so much with the detail of the earth life, you obscure the path that leads upwards and remain rooted in a horizontal plane, or path, that goes nowhere, except that it gives you an opportunity to experience different kinds of wilderness. Awaken and open your hearts to the certain knowledge that what I tell you is truth.

When you surrender you give up attachment. You may continue the earth life, going to the office, and that sort of routine, but you should become immune to events that take place within that confine and be unaffected by them. Do not concern yourself with the outcome of what is going on, leave others who care more about those things to concern themselves with all that. You should become the witness, like the Lord who is always happy. The success or failure of any effort does not enter into the spiritual attitude because the whole of the earth life is a game.

Long periods of meditation are good, a chance to reach up to the higher levels and experience an intimate feeling of union with God during those quiet moments when all worldly thoughts fall away. Leave the earth life to others and just do your best in whatever situation you find yourself. Do not concern yourself with the results.

You worry all the time, worry about everything, but none of these things should concern you. Just do what you have to do at the time and put all worrying thoughts out of your mind. At present your mind is full of worries, about this and that. Forget it all and only concern yourself with the present. Leave all the rest to the Lord.

Life will change, soon, but you have to prepare yourself so that you are ready to take full advantage of the opportunities which will come. There is nothing to fear. What comes is the result of the past and will bring a clarification of much which you do not now understand. You will experience the truth, that all is God and that there is only God. It will be a revelation which will touch you deeply.

Awaken, My child, forget the past, all that is behind you. The new golden age dawns and you will experience that richness of life which is only possible when you reach the higher levels of consciousness.

Surrender today and open the door to the in-flowing of the God force so that it reaches the innermost part of your being. It is there within, it is there without, and when you surrender you allow the two to join in perfect unison. From that moment onwards you live in perfect harmony with God. Nothing can then touch you.

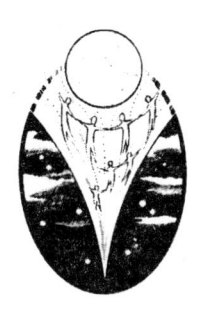

## OMNIPRESENCE

I am the Lord of the universe. Have implicit faith in Me for I am you and you are Me. I am with you now, with you always, inside you, outside you, everywhere. I am your sunshine and your shadow. So blend with Me, harmonise with Me, the divine giver of life, the divine supporter of life, the only source of life, the very omnipresence that you often talk about. That is what it is. You can deny Me, you can despise Me, you can ignore Me, but I will always be with you for I am within your very heart. I am part of you, I *am* you and you are part of Me. Those are words of truth and wisdom.

Many know it intellectually but very few behave as though they believe it. Bad habits continue, there are jealousies, weaknesses of character, in fact, all those weaknesses that you must learn to overcome.

Today you are gathered here [for the satsang] in complete harmony. Maintain that harmony when you leave and work together for harmony in the whole world. Look for Me everywhere. Feel My presence now, in this very room. Just pause and know that I am here.

I will help you, all of you, for each one of you is helping My mission in one way or another. Do not look back even though many mistakes have been made. Live now, live every moment of every day, live in the present and surrender to the will of God.

Ask yourself, who is this little me that has so many wants and desires of one kind or another? Where is it all leading me?

I bless you all. I am with you now and will always be with you. Never doubt that or have any fear.

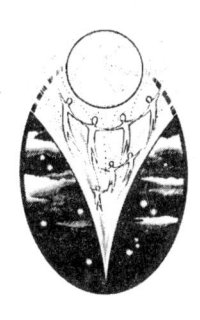

## INNER CONTROL

It is good that you talk to My children for their needs are great.

There can be no peace or tranquillity in the minds of those whose lives are ruled by desire. In such a state how can anyone expect to find happiness, let alone peace of mind, for in that state the mind is simply a web of desires.

Self-examination is the only way to overcome this problem. Take a deep look into the soul to find that soul and see what it is that is causing the disturbance. Analyse each thought that comes and each individual desire. What is it that you really want in this life? How is it that you can want anything once you reach the level of the pure soul which is the real you, the God within?

To look within is the only solution to so many of your problems. Most of you spend your time looking outwards and blaming others, or even God Himself for all your woes!

The true path is neither easy nor difficult, it is simply the only path that will lead you to peace and tranquillity and eventual reunion with God. Every one of you here today should take a decision to examine yourself thoroughly and then make a vow to move away from every form of earthly desire and start a new life along the spiritual path. The Ceiling on Desires programme will help you to make that start.

I will always be waiting for you at the end of the path and I will be watching every step that you take. I am with you, each one of you, every moment of the day, for I reside in your heart. I will always be there to help anyone who turns to Me in true humility and with a pure heart.

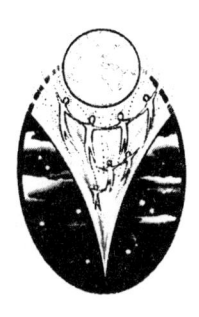

## CONTEMPLATING THE TRUTH

When you gather together in My name, there is a gathering of kindred souls, people who have chosen to tread the spiritual path and seek the ultimate truth which is God the Absolute.

It should be a time of quiet meditation, when you contemplate the truth, for it is in these moments, when many are gathered together, that the God force flows and makes it easier for you to be aware of It and all It stands for. In these moments, all worldly cares are put aside and thoughts are on the spiritual plane. Meditate on this and know that I am with you.

Try to have a short period of quiet meditation during the meeting, perhaps just a few minutes, when you can all sit in complete silence and experience the God force welling up from the heart of each one of you. The experience will be refreshing and invigorating.!

I will be there, I am always there. Sometimes you are aware of My presence, sometimes not, it depends on your own state and the level at which you are manifesting yourself at that time.

When love flows, it is My love and that is the easiest way to find Me. I send My love to each one of you.

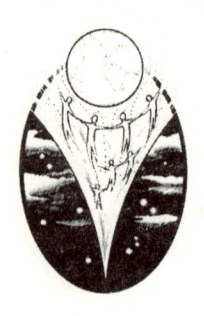

## THE SAI ORGANISATION

Harmony and the Sai organisation... What is all this?

Harmony arises when kindred souls blossom together like flowers blossoming in the garden. There is a sense of unity as they all grow together.

What is the Sai organisation? It is simply a gathering together of souls who have started to become awakened to truth.

The Sai organisation should be motivated by love.

You join the organisation both to give, to receive, to progress, to learn, to become inspired and to serve.

The organisation itself is not important, it exists only for what it gives: an opportunity for searching souls to gather together and find the way to progress along the spiritual path and to help others on the same journey.

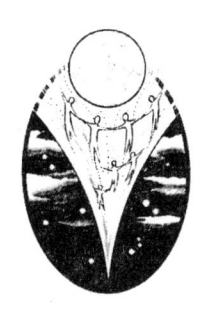

## SPIRITUAL EFFORT (II)

My children, My children, if only you knew how much I love you all. You should love Me as I love you and then so many of your problems would disappear. Yes, love Me, love everyone, and experience the wonderful cleansing of your soul as love, which is the life force itself, flows through you.

Life without love is life without God and is akin to living in a world without light. And until you experience true love, you have not experienced anything. Life without love is simply illusion, a life without any form of lasting fulfilment or happiness.

Change does not come overnight, but change can be set in motion at this very moment. And once the change is set in motion, the momentum will increase as each day passes. But old habits die hard and great determination is required to bring about the change. I am always there to help you if you turn to Me. Take just one step towards Me and I will take a hundred towards you, but you must make the first move. Is that not a solution to many of your problems? However, man has free will and nothing will happen unless he exercises that free will.

Awaken, My children, and see the light that shines so strongly once you open your eyes. Leave behind that life of illusion and know that such a life can never lead you anywhere except into a state of deeper and deeper despair. Start afresh today and determine to live your life in harmony with God, so that you can claim your real inheritance as a child of the living God, a manifestation of God Himself.

Rise up to the higher levels of consciousness, and know that if you truly follow the teachings of the Lord, then peace will come into your life and you will experience the bliss of unity which is divinity itself, the ultimate state being the total merging, or union, with God where you and God are one.

My children, I wait for you patiently while My love flows constantly all over the world.

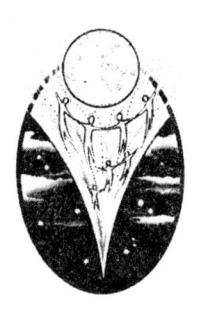

## SURRENDER (II)

When the wind blows, it is a sign that changes are on the way. Nothing lasts for ever, even the universe is in a constant state of change and man himself plays a part in those changes.

Now is a time of much activity and movement and it is important to be involved and to play a part. Each one should examine his position in the world and consider whether he is playing out the right part. There are so many opportunities.

Man should have a regular dialogue with God and move forward with the God force which is always moving.

Change, movement... do not resist those changes, do not be disturbed when the past is no more and old habits no longer seem appropriate for the present and the future. Man gets into such a routine, usually of a type that will never get him anywhere.

In some cases, it is as though the "handbrake" is clutched so firmly all the time in an effort to hang on to the past at all cost, really only due to a fear of insecurity and worry about the future. But what is there to fear when you place yourself totally in the hands of the Lord?

Surrender is the only solution that brings peace. Dissociate yourself from the past, that was a life without God, and let go of all feeling of resistance. Be convinced that the Lord will look after you in everything that you do. Laugh when the outcome is different to the one you expected, and be happy at all times. See the little problems for what they are: passing trivialities.

Even about.............., what does it matter? Leave it to the Lord.

My child, be patient, just wait and see and accept whatever comes. These little aggravations should not worry or disturb you so much.

Give Me your love and see how My love will pour out and fill you with ecstasy. That is fulfilment, the Lord's love.

You will never find fulfilment in business affairs or anything else.

Look for inner peace and it will come. It is not so far away.

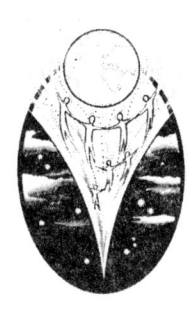

## THE INNER TEACHER

Truth emerges and flows from the heart, the soul, the God within, the inner consciousness, the source, all of which are God, and represent all truth, all love, a total oneness.

That is the only truth and it is inseparable because it is one and the whole. All else is illusion or a form of illusion.

Why do you meditate? To reach inside and release the God within so that you and God become one. Then perfect peace flows and all worldly problems and desires cease to exist.

As the years go by, all of you should draw closer to God by identifying yourselves with Him and realising the truth, living the truth, putting aside illusion, desire and ignorance.

Live in God, live with God, be God, know that all is God and that there is only God. That is the whole truth and that is also the challenge!

Meditate on those thoughts and then contemplate who is this little me who seems so lost, lost because so many of you have lost your very identity, and yet all you need to do is to stop and contemplate the truth.

When you find the truth, know the truth, live the truth, then you and God are really one. At this point the little me can be put to rest for ever more; yes, that little me with all its worries, its ego, desires, greed, envy, jealousy and every negative attitude. Do you really want to continue living on that level?

Think about it and remember the truth... I AM.

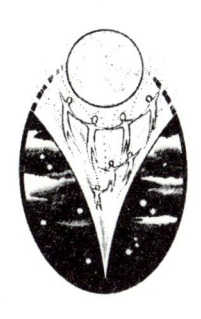

## TIME (I)

What is today? It is the passage of time.

The earth revolves on its axis and continues its motion which was started millions of years ago. It is a demonstration of perfect unison and inter-related activity which exists throughout the universe, all part of the whole, everything relating to everything else, everything and every motion affecting everything else.

You are part of that whole, that pattern, and your activities and thoughts affect the whole.

How few people realise this truth; for, if they did, how could they behave the way they do, caring only for themselves, their pleasures, comfort and personal security? But the law applies to all and your life and life pattern affect many others, even those who you do not know and perhaps will never see.

Behind all this activity is the omnipresent Lord, the Creator, the Life Force, the unity within the whole, and the force that manifests as each one of you, each animal, each plant, each insect, every stone. They are all Mine and part of the whole.

It is the realisation of this basic truth that should galvanise man into action, action to rectify the past, action to purify the present and fructify the future. This is where My devotees should play a part and spread the message far and wide. It is the duty of the more awakened ones to lead the others forward so that they too may play a more active part in My work and My mission.

At all times all of you should draw your energy and inspiration from the Lord through moments, or periods, of quiet meditation, when you can establish close communication with the Lord. At these moments a divine peace will come over you and divine inspiration will flow.

Time is precious but in your lives so much time is wasted, even a whole lifetime may be frittered away pursuing material and pleasurable pursuits which are not only selfish but lead you nowhere. You must overcome the desire of the flesh, and desire only God, unity, love and harmony.

The starting point should be service to humanity, for that will turn your mind away from self and the personal desires of the moment. It is the best starting point for most people, although quiet meditation is the path for others, meditation which will awaken the inner soul and lead it forward to positive action. Once you know the truth, how can anyone delay this action any longer?

Sadly, most of you are so immersed in the illusion of material life that the realisation of divinity does not come easily. It is shrouded by layers of thick cloud, the result of the past and the present, because your own mental processes have chosen to obscure the truth so that you can continue to enjoy, as you imagine, material and sensual pleasures of the earth life. But this is not the purpose of the earth life and that is not the reason why you have incarnated at this time.

Your life, this birth, is a challenge and you have the opportunity to accept that challenge and turn way from illusion for ever more. The Kingdom of Heaven is not far away, and that kingdom is within you now. Look inside and taste the bliss of the true divine life. Follow the path that will lead you to the permanent divine state and liberation.

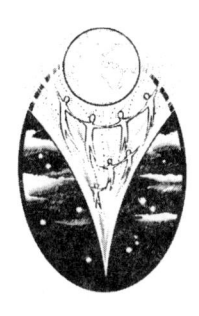

## TIME (II)

Time is a manifestation of life, but time is also timeless. You measure time by the clock and relate it to day and night on your planet, which itself turns continuously on its own axis. Elsewhere in the universe there is constant movement, but time, as you understand it, does not exist.

There is confusion in the mind of man because time on your planet has become so important and you cannot conceive the timeless state. But it is there, always has been and always will be.

Time is now, and NOW is the time for action. Swami speaks like this in the hope that man can be awakened in this lifetime. You can remember Swami saying (at the interview when He pointed at my wristwatch), "Watch has no value but time has much value, do not waste that time and do what you can NOW."

Time is passing, time is precious, the time of the present moment, as you understand it, can never come back once it has passed. It is like a history book, full of the story of life, year by year. Your life is like that. You can look back, the past is in the past, but you have free will to write your own history book from this point onwards. What will that book look like in five or ten years' time? It depends on you and what decisions you take NOW.

Every moment is NOW, every moment is vital and every moment wasted is lost for ever. Once you are awakened, every moment becomes more and more precious, moments when you can draw closer and closer to the Lord. Even now, in spite of so much understanding, God comes very low in your priorities of life. That is wrong, you should reverse your priorities and put God first and the world and all its activities second. Then you would find peace, for peace can only be found through God, and the path to God is through love and service.

Change comes to everyone, sometimes quickly, sometimes slowly, but change is always taking place even when you are not aware of it. Nothing stands still because the universe is in a constant state of change and you are part of that whole. Stagnation is only an apparent state. It is a transient state of illusion.

NOW is the time for change, change of vibration, change of thought pattern, change of values, change of ideals, change of levels of consciousness. It can be achieved through closer links and better communication with God. I am that God, I am here, open to every thought. So, how can you put aside the chance to be at one with Me in this lifetime? If you really try, you can lift yourself out of the denseness of materialism and rise to the highest levels of consciousness, where you can experience unity with the Lord Himself. It is a process which requires constant practice, daily meditation and a continuing dialogue with the Lord. NOW is the time to start. Put aside all worldly desires and reach out to the Lord. He is always there, waiting patiently for you.

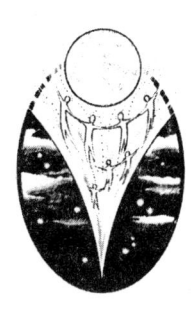

## CREATOR, CREATURE AND CREATION

I created the universe and I created your world, as you know it.

I created man in My own image, a manifestation of God in human form. It was My leela, but with a purpose, an expression of My love which is so limitless that it must express and manifest itself at all times. It is an ever expanding force, My love, a force more powerful than anything else that exists, for love itself is God, or a manifestation of God. God is formless but God has form. You cannot understand this, nor can anyone else, nor can you understand Me. One moment I am human with form, behaving like a man or a woman, and simultaneously I am manifest as God everywhere in the universe, for, truly, there is only God and different manifestations and forms of God.

I created man with free will and there was a purpose. I always knew what would happen. It is all part of a perfect plan, impossible for man to understand in all its detail and beauty. But man was overcome by greed and desire, and has reached the very threshold of destroying the world. It is at this point that I incarnate in human form, not to save the world, for I could do that with a wave of My hand, but to show man the way to save his own world. This again is God's leela, that man shall have free will and hence only man will be allowed to save his world. I will show the way and will send many people to help in the task. You and many others are among them.

But it will not be easy and it will take time.

I Myself am in the middle of a triple incarnation and, even now, only the seeds are sown. But divine seeds bear divine fruit and My plan is perfect, so do not doubt or fear.

Man is indeed imperfect, the product of his own creation and undoing. But all that will eventually change and, when that happens, man will once again live in peace and harmony. Love and peace will return to the earth and cleanse the horrors and excesses of the dark ages which today pollute the very atmosphere.

What can you do to help? Be like a beacon in the sky, radiating love and light, that is what you and everyone else can do for the Lord. Only through love can the world be saved.

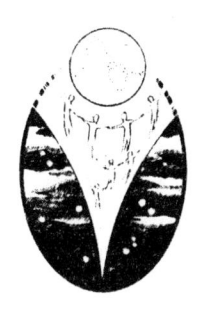

## UNITY IN ACTION

Concentrate on the omnipresence of the Lord, UNITY, and the fact that all are one. Only then can you get all other thoughts into perspective. This is the background to both education and service, for omnipresence is the whole basis of life in all its aspects.

When you experience omnipresence, you should live for Sai and realise that there is nothing else.

Turn to Sai, think Sai, live Sai, love Sai, do everything for Sai, then peace will come and love will flow. This is the solution to all your problems.

What is the Sai organisation doing? Sadly, not enough, but a beginning has been made and all of you should now make the effort to work together and expand the activities. Success will come if you work hard enough and if you continually turn your thoughts to God, concentrating on helping others and forgetting about self. That is true surrender.

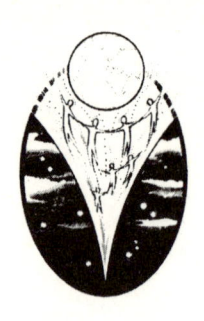

## UNITY (II)

All are one and you must always remember this.

But it is also important to spread My message to the West and it is right to make a special effort to do this, now that more people are becoming aware of My presence and the message that I bring.

Never rush into anything. Even the truth unfolds slowly. Just continue to draw people to your group, as they emerge and encourage others to start small groups, in the same way that you have done. A pattern will emerge and more and more people will appear. It is like the opening of a lotus. When conditions are right it opens and it carries a special symbolic meaning, the opening out and spreading of the word of God in all directions in an atmosphere of divine bliss.

I am always at the centre of the lotus, the source of the love, wisdom and beauty which pours out and attracts those souls who are sufficiently awakened. You are channels in that process.

Do not ignore anyone for all are Mine. Just do your best for everyone and never worry about the outcome.

Many are not ready but have simply joined the Sai movement, not really knowing what it is that they want. They are still lost in the wilderness, but at least it is a beginning and you have to help and encourage them.

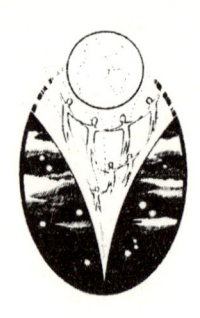

## LEVELS OF CONSCIOUSNESS

What is upliftment? It is the rising up of the soul to a higher level of consciousness. Who is it who controls this level? You do, for you have that free will to rise above the grosser levels and to manifest yourself at even the highest levels of consciousness. But few people make any serious effort to break away from the grosser material levels and the habits they have developed over so many years. It needs a sudden wrench, something traumatic to galvanise man into action. But it is never too late, and every day that man continues on the old path is a day wasted.

What can you do? Stop now and contemplate the past, the present and the future. Has the past been satisfactory? What about the present? And what will the future be like if you continue without change? It will just be a repetition of the same old pattern, a slow road to nowhere, and with no sense of fulfilment.

So if you want upliftment, spend more time in communion with the Lord, for it is in that state that you can prepare yourself for the future and then move onto new ground and reach the higher levels of consciousness. This is the only way to find true peace and happiness and achieve a feeling of fulfilment which will satisfy the soul.

It is a gradual process and it will only begin when you make the first move. The time for that move is now!

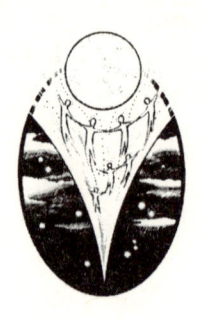

## CREATION

In the beginning there was nothing, just an endless void, but I was always there, the origin, the true beginning.

But, really, there was no beginning, as I always was, always have been and always will be. That is the true mystery of God, impossible for man to understand.

I am love, all love, total love, and love itself is God. It was the continual outpouring of this love that brought about the creation of the world, a playground where I could express My love and watch it spread like a fire which begins in the tinder wood. Nothing can stop it.

The creation of man is the re-creation of Myself in My own image. You are that creation and you are all My children. That is why every detail about each one of you is known to Me, even every thought.

It is My leela, My creation, My joy, My love, and an expression of My omnipresence. But behind all this is a plan, My plan, and that too is something which man cannot understand. This is the mystery of God and it will always remain.

That, My child, is the truth and you should think about it and see how you relate to it. Man should contemplate the mystery of God even if he cannot understand it, and he should adjust his life according to his own interpretation of the meaning and purpose of life itself.

It is part of God's plan to let His children work out their own destiny and salvation, culminating in eventual liberation and reunion with God Himself. This is the inevitable result of life. The passage represents an experience of illusion, or apparent separation from God, whereas, in truth, all is God and always has been, for there is nothing in the universe which is not God or the creation of God.

Love is the message for everyone. Love is the most potent force in the universe, for love is truly the manifestation of God Himself.

Let this love flow all around you, inside and outside, and then you will prepare the way for liberation and at the same time help many other souls on the same path.

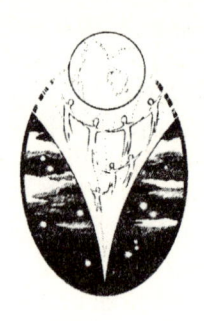

## UNITY (III)

**W**hen the sun shines, open your mind to the concept of UNITY, because you can see the sun which is the source of light, heat and energy on earth. It is a link with the whole universe. You look into the sky and you see a star, your own sun. Then you should visualise what lies beyond, the vast universe, unlimited, and everything therein vibrating and moving in perfect harmony and unison.

Look out on a clear night and observe the Milky Way, a vast galaxy of stars thousands of light years away, and yet, this is only the threshold of the universe. My child, the vastness of the universe is beyond man's concept, and always will be; neither can the scientists comprehend the miracle which they observe in just one tiny area.

Here is the manifestation of the Lord, Lord of the Cosmos, the Creator, the Unifier, the One and the Whole.

Stop for a moment and marvel at the thought that you and the Creator are one and the same, all One, all God, all part of that monumental WHOLE.

You have the choice to manifest yourself as part of that whole, in the divine Godlike state, or to live a body-life, where you identify with your body and thereby lose your real identity. So many do this and then wonder why they are lost, unhappy and unsatisfied. But you will never find lasting happiness through the body-life.

So, turn your thoughts to the Divine. Contemplate the omnipresence of the Lord. Know that you and He are one and that He is beside you, within you, all around you, now and always.

Decide today to manifest yourself as Godman, in the divine state, and live your life from now on as though you were God Himself.

Contemplate every action, every thought, as though you were God. Then peace and lasting happiness will come to you and you will help to bring peace and happiness to the world and to all around you.

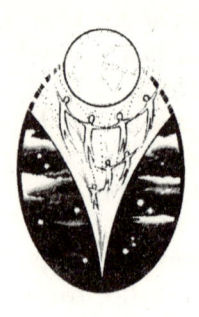

## CONFIDENCE

Where is the love, the love that pours from the heavens, the source, the fountain head, the Godhead, call it which ever name you like?

Stop and consider where it is at this moment in relation to yourself. How do you feel? Tired, worn out, no energy, utterly exhausted before the day begins. Why is this? It means you are closed off, separated from the source and it is you yourself who have put up a barrier for one reason or another.

Even at this moment you can smell the sweet fragrance of jasmine, a manifestation of the love that pours out from the heavens. There is no separation from the source in this case.

Open your hearts and they will be filled with love, My love, and then you will be recharged with superhuman energy.

Breathe in My love and My energy and feel your whole being vibrating in perfect harmony with the universe and with God Himself. This is the secret of good health, good living and boundless energy. All of you should do the same and transform your lives into a more vibrant state, so that you can fulfil the task for which you have incarnated.

Never look on the dark side of anything, regardless of the apparent gravity of the situation. Turn to God, to the source, breathe in the sweet love and divine energy that fill the universe. Laugh in happiness and experience the bliss of being at one with God.

All worldly problems will simply melt away and be seen to be what they really are: nothing more than stones on the path. You have the ability to walk over those stones and leave them behind you for ever more.

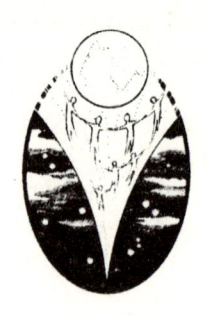

## UNITY (IV)

Purity, unity and divinity are the foundations of the universe. All are ONE and I am the WHOLE. There is nothing that exists outside that WHOLE and that is the meaning of unity. Everyone is part of that WHOLE, an enormous unlimited spiritual power and force which exists throughout the universe.

The fuel for that force is LOVE, and that love is God manifesting in everyone and everything.

Unity comes to a community or group of people when love flows. Flowers need water for nourishment and man needs love to sustain him and enable him to fulfil his task in the world. What is that task? It begins with the realisation of his true nature, his real identity, because only when he knows who he is can he progress on the spiritual path.

What is love? Love is God. Where is that love now? God is omnipresent, everywhere, in everyone and everything so that love is here, there and everywhere. But you have to release it and allow that love to flow, like the rivers. Man creates great dams on the earth to control the natural flow of water, and man too in his ignorance creates the same type of barrier which restricts the free flow of love. Hence you have all these troubles on the earth, in the world: man fighting man, nation fighting nation, the result of total ignorance on the part of man.

But God is there always, the same God who has given free will to man. God watches, God observes, God waits and God alone understands the timeless nature of life and the true meaning of eternity.

My children, awaken and release that divine love that is locked within you, within the heart. Know that God is in you and that you are part of God, part of the whole, manifesting and vibrating as an aspect of God Himself. See everyone else in the same light, all God, all part of the same whole. Then unity will return to the earth and a new generation will be born. That day will come. You are the instruments, and each one of you has a unique opportunity to participate in the work of the Lord. Accept that challenge today and become beacons of love and light which will brighten the dark skies all around you for ever more.

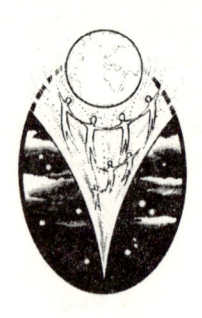

## DIVINE DESIGN

**M**y child, out of turmoil will come peace and tranquillity – it is the will of the Lord.

You give far too much importance to the minor disturbances on the surface of the sea and are oblivious to the vast whole of the ocean which is out of sight.

See everything in that light: the things that worry you are all little local disturbances or draughts.

I am aware of everything that goes on, good and bad, and I know how everything will eventually fall into place. Changes will come quite soon if you are patient.

Everyone fits into what you would call a giant jigsaw puzzle and you are the pieces. Some pieces are jagged but even they fit in perfectly when the final pattern of the picture emerges. So it will be with the Sai organisation and everyone will have played a part. The long process of putting the puzzle together is an exercise which is good for all of you. It brings out your weaknesses and gives you a chance to polish that diamond which is the core of your being. Only when the diamond is purified can you re-enter the kingdom of heaven, the abode of perfect peace.

Do not give so much importance to all the aggravation.

Just play out the game and know that there is a reason and purpose behind everything. Calmer waters always follow the storm. Tranquillity is not far away, so do not despair. This is an opportunity for all of you and you must not waste it.

Life is a game. You must see it like that and look upon everyone as players. Each one has a part to play, just like you and all the others.

Consider the life of Jesus and those around him. They were not all saints or very spiritual people, but they all played a part in the game which was being played out at that time. It goes on and on, from generation to generation, and the hand of the Lord is always there at the helm.

Life will change, it will improve and you will experience a richness in the quality of life which has eluded you in the past.

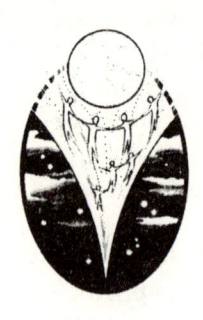

## BEING

Look up into the heavens and observe the universe in all its glory. Look into your own heart and know that it is the house of the Lord, for He is omnipresent and resides there.

Consider the purpose of your life. Meditate on the lessons you have learned and contemplate the way ahead.

Man tends to make some progress and then stagnate, not knowing where to go beyond that point. But the path ahead is always there, right in front of him, the path that leads through service to humanity towards a closer and closer relationship with God, for all humanity is God.

Never concern yourself with the ups and downs of daily life, for these are like the waves of the ocean. They come, they go, and so it is with daily life. The traumas of the day, when they come, eventually pass. Observe them but do not become involved in them. Look on them as a passing pattern, nothing of permanent consequence.

But man is permanent for man is an eternal being. Contemplate that thought and try to purify your whole life. Purity, unity and divinity are the very pillars of life itself.

Man is confused at the present time but the dawn of awakening is at hand. Retain that thought in your mind, that happier times lie ahead, and do not become part of the confusion that surrounds you.

Turn to God in moments of despair, knowing that God alone is the permanent guiding light in your life, never affected by anything, never wavering, just like the brightest star in the sky, always shining for everyone to see.

You need to develop those qualities so that you too shine like another bright star and become a reflection of the God within manifesting at the highest level.

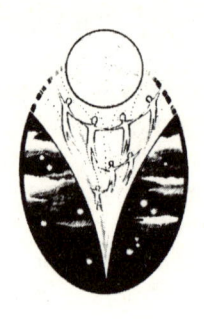

## EFFORT

There is confusion in the mind of man caused by the separation he has chosen, that is, separation from God, separation from the source, separation from the very supplier of everything that man needs.

Due to ignorance, desire and the animal instincts, which have yet to be overcome, man treads another path, far away from the spiritual, or divine path which is in reality the only path. All other paths are simply illusion and lead to a wilderness which is where man resides at present.

Now is the time for man to awaken to the truth: that all is God and man is part of that whole, as are his mother and his brother, his friends and his enemies – all are one, all children of God Almighty.

Only when man realises the truth can change come about and only then is he likely to emerge from the wilderness, move away from the material path and take the first steps that will lead him towards divinity.

It is the duty of those awakened ones to spread the message, the message of truth, so that more and more people become awakened. It may not be easy but much progress can be made from small beginnings. Already a start has been made and progress will continue. Very soon new openings will appear and you must take all the opportunities as they arise. The meetings of the various Sai groups are a great help and slowly the people will become more and more inspired by and convinced of the truth. As the truth unfolds, more people will accept the challenge and start their own groups.

That is what is required, more Sai groups, rather than the same people just continuing to go to other people's groups, imagining that this is all that is required of them.

Encourage the members of your own group to start their own little Study Circles, even two or three people, and slowly a whole new pattern will emerge. I will always be there to help those who make the effort.

Open your hearts and listen to the voice of the Lord who is calling you like a shepherd calling to his flock. Know that I am always there, even if you do not see Me. Even the sheep know that the shepherd is not far away though they may not see him, so how can you doubt the omnipresence of your own shepherd, the Lord who is always with you, always has been and always will be, even though you may deny Him?

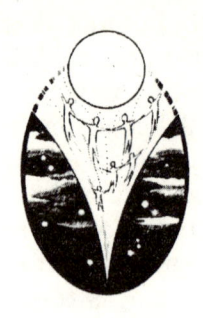

## THE AIM OF LIFE

Swami's life is Swami's message.

You should contemplate the life style of the Lord and compare your own way of life to see where you go wrong. The reasons are clear: desire and conflicting aims.

Consider what it is that you are trying to achieve in this life. Consider, too, how much time you are wasting on trivial matters that are of no lasting importance.

Create a new plan of life and a new life pattern. Do not let trivial affairs interfere with that plan. Have a definite objective and determine to achieve it. Do not make the plan too ambitious to start with; think in terms of phases, and set a time scale to achieve phase one.

There is always a tendency just to exist and let time pass, but this is not the right way to live, it is time wasted, life wasted. As you get older, time becomes even more precious and it must not be wasted.

Day to day life can continue, but never forget the purpose of life and your relationship with the Lord. It is so easy to drift into habit, the same pattern day after day, and this is one way in which life gets wasted.

Analyse the present position: where have you got to and where are you going? What is it that delays your progress on the spiritual path?.

Only you can work out the future pattern of your own life.

Look for happiness, see it all around you, the sight of God manifesting everywhere, in the flowers, in the plants, in the trees, in the people and in the animals. All are God, all are one, all part of the whole. It is that thought that should be constantly in your mind, the unity that exists throughout the universe, the unity that is divinity.

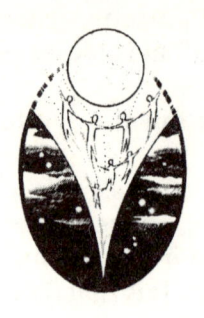

## A CHRISTMAS MESSAGE FOR THE SAI CHILDREN

My children, I love you all and you should love Me as I love you!

Do not separate yourselves from God, for you yourselves are God. We are all one happy family and I am the Mother and the Father of all of you.

Purity, unity, divinity, these three are inseparable, so you should strive to find and develop these qualities at all times. Learn from an early age not to be distracted by the desires of the senses, for these will delay your progress on the spiritual path, especially if you allow them to get hold of you while you are still young. The older you are, the more difficult it becomes to overcome these desires which grow like a cancer if allowed to go unchecked over a long period.

But, My children, you are still young and you have a whole lifetime ahead of you, a life with Sai and a golden opportunity to achieve pure divinity in this lifetime.

Celebrate this Christmas, but also use it as a time for contemplation, a time to realise the truth, a time to contemplate your future; whether it is to be a life with Sai, which will lead you forward to liberation from bondage, or a life which is controlled by the desires of the senses, a life which will lead you nowhere.

Realise the great truth that we are all one, all God, and that the body is simply a temporary vehicle for the soul.

Live with God, live in God, be God, and then you will find peace, happiness, fulfilment and eventual liberation.

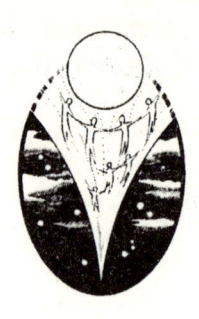

## CHRISTMAS MESSAGE (1983)

What is Christmas?

It should be a time of divine awakening, a time when people turn their thoughts away from everyday problems and think instead of the divine. That spirit of the divine is everywhere and you yourselves are part of it. Learn to live in that divine state.

Follow the light and experience the omnipresence of the Lord. Let Christmas be a time of awakening for each one of you.

Live in peace, live in love, look for love everywhere, for it is the manifestation of God Himself. Love one another, help one another, that is the path to divinity.

I am always with you and aware of every thought; so, when you know this and understand it, surely you will turn away from the constant obsession with material things and every form of desire.

The dawn of the Golden Age is at hand but not everyone will experience it. The age of preparation precedes the Golden Age and it is during this time that the sorting out process takes place. So seize the opportunity that all of you have been given to rise above the material level and manifest once again in the divine state. Only then can you enter the Golden Age and experience the omnipresence of the Lord.

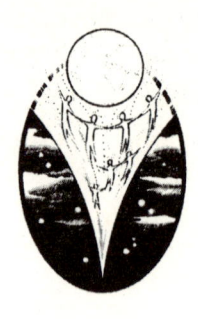

## CHRISTMAS MESSAGE (1984)

When you celebrate Christmas, the birth of Christ, you should celebrate also your own birth and the fact that you are here on earth in this form.

Christmas should be a time of self-examination. Christ came 2,000 years ago to awaken man to the truth. Today the Sai Avatar is here with the same message. It is such an opportunity that you have and yet so few of you are taking it. How many have really become awakened? How many have really changed their life style as a result of My teachings? How many of you are motivated by love in all that you do? The Lord cannot be deceived.

My children, awaken before it is too late. The present life comes and goes and time passes ever more quickly. What are you doing as each day passes? Are you really changing your way of life and moving away from earth-bound darkness into the light, back towards the Godhead?

I am with you always, in your midst, so you do not even need to come to India to find Me. Find Me here today, in your heart, ever present, and consider the truth that you and God are one. When you know this, your way of life will change as well as your attitude towards those around you, for they too are My children.

Celebrate Christmas, celebrate your own presence on the earth, and then come to terms with the truth of who you really are. Celebrate the wonderful opportunity that lies ahead in the light of that understanding and start afresh on a new path: the only path that will lead you out of the wilderness and back to the Godhead, where liberation and the total merging of the soul with God bring divine bliss.

In the process, as you move along that path, you should become a great beacon of light, lighting up the path so that others can also find the way. This is the highest form of personal sadhana.

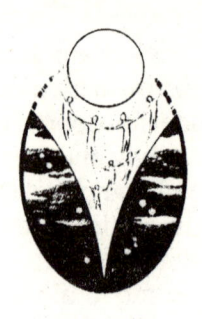

## EDUCATION IN HUMAN VALUES

What is life? It is a manifestation of God in different forms. Life is life in any form, all a part of God and divinity. Life is at many levels of consciousness and man on earth can reach the highest level. But this is only possible after a long struggle during which man learns to master the senses. So long as man is ruled by his senses he cannot move very far along the spiritual path because his whole mind revolves round himself and this will simply lead him nowhere or, at best, round in circles.

Man must break out of this circle and move forward. But this is possible only after he decides to make a great effort to break the ties that bind him so firmly to the material way of life, where his senses always hold sway. So it is partly a question of educating himself, for until he learns the truth, he is unlikely to make much effort to change.

This is where education in human values begins, TRUTH. Once you learn the truth and begin to live the truth, you are on the right path. Where does truth lead you? It leads to the ultimate realisation that all is God and there is only God, and that you are part of the whole which is God.

As the truth unfolds, so your attitude will change and you

will begin to change your way of life towards right living or righteousness. You will begin to treat everyone else as they really are, part of the whole, all divine, all God. You will begin to love them and by loving them learn to love yourself for until you love yourself, you cannot escape from insecurity and the disturbed mind which accompanies this negative state.

Love will begin to blossom and peace will follow, peace of mind leading to tranquillity when you can experience the true feeling that you and God are one. Life thereafter will be totally different for it becomes a spiritual life instead of a material one. All is love, all is God, all is peace and all is divine.

There is only one path, the path that leads back to God. The signposts are there, if only you open your eyes. It is the only way ahead.

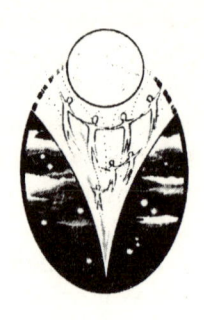

## COURAGE

You need courage in life to achieve anything worthwhile. Courage results from faith in the Lord and leads to certainty that anything can be achieved if it is the will of the Lord. Therefore, the first thing which you should determine is the correct path to take in life. Where are you now, where are you going and where do you want to go?

If you put your faith in the Lord and pray earnestly to Him, He will guide you and you will reach the goal. Courage leads to certainty, and vice versa.

Time is important in life because each life on earth is unique, it can never be quite the same again.

Life leads to life and eventually to life everlasting, eternal life in the liberated state. That is a permanent state of bliss when you and God become one. It is the state of "I AM".

Experience all aspects of the earth life while you are there and clarify their true values in your mind so that you reach an understanding of what is real, and what is temporary and a form of illusion. It is a way to discover yourself, for in the end you will find that only you are real and all else is illusion.

At the end of this life you should have the certain

knowledge, understanding and experience of "I AM". I and God are one. Liberation follows from the moment that you reach the permanent state of "I AM" because, at that point, all else, all desire, all illusion and all feeling, emotional and physical, simply drop away and cease to be reality. It is a state of the purified soul where all duality has gone and there is only unity, unity with God, and the permanent state of bliss.

Reach for that goal and devote the rest of your life to achieving it. I will help you.

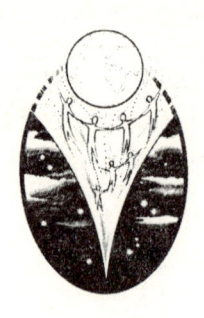

# FAITH

**M**y child, I am always with you, you need never doubt that, even in your darkest moments.

The sea has many moods as you saw last night (watching television), but always there are periods of calm in the same way that happiness is a period between two pains. See the whole world like this, see your own lives like this and welcome all difficulties as further experiences necessary for your own development and good.

When you evolve further along the path, either these difficulties will not come into your lives any more, or your reaction to them will be entirely neutral and they will no longer affect you, emotionally or in any other way.

What are these problems that disturb you so much? Insecurity is behind them, lack of faith in yourself and doubt about your ability to overcome worldly difficulties. There is ego too, and you wonder how all this will affect you.

All this needs continuous examination until you reach the point where you know that you and God are one, and then nothing will disturb or distress you.

Meditate upon these thoughts: know that I am there at all times; talk to Me more often and put your trust in Me and then the quality of your life will improve.

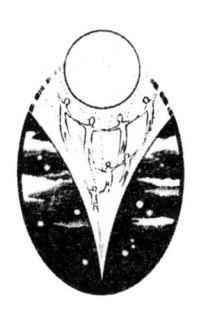

## NEW YEAR (1983)

This will be a year of great progress and I would like to see each one of you participating in that progress. What is progress? It is spiritual development, development of the soul on the long path that leads to divinity. So many of you have been sitting on the sidelines for too long, waiting for something... waiting for what? You don't know, so you continue the long wait. But I have arrived to awaken you and I am here with you now, here with each and every one of you.

AWAKEN, AWAKEN, as the New Year begins to unfold, and remember that I will be with you every single day of the year. So, how can you sit idly and pretend any longer that you are waiting for something before taking action? I have arrived. I am here now and I will never leave. Contemplate these thoughts when you first wake up in the morning, dwell on them during the day, and remember them before you fall asleep at night. Resolve to live in harmony with all around you, to live in a state of perfect peace, to love everyone and to dedicate your life to the service of fellow man. That is the pathway to divinity and everlasting peace.

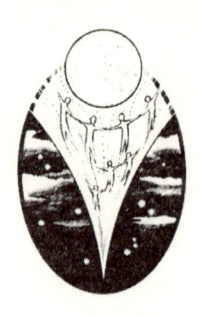

*BIRTHDAY MESSAGE NOVEMBER 1982*

## BIRTH DAY

I am the Lord of the Universe, the Creator, and I have created each one of you individually, hence I know and recognise each one of you when you come to see me in India. I know all about you. I am with each one of you now so I know the thoughts of every single person, as well as what you were thinking yesterday and the day before. Watch your thoughts because it is through these thoughts that you create your own future.

I created you in a state of perfection because you are part of Me. But, during the passage of many lives, you are tossed about by the waves of life and you lose your awareness of divinity. As you get lost, you get more and more drawn away by the materialistic attractions of life in the flesh, life with body, life on earth, and you get more and more confused. Then quite suddenly, comes the awakening and it may come at any time. This is the rebirth, the reawakening to the awareness of the divinity within. When this awareness comes, how can you possibly desire anything, except to reach out for God and merge in Him once again, thus experiencing true divinity and perfect bliss?

There will be many temptations on this arduous path but these experiences will prepare you for the long journey ahead.

On this auspicious day, realise that it is a day of rebirth, a chance of rebirth for each one of you. Look at your desires and cravings. Examine them one by one and take a positive decision to cut them out and eliminate them during the course of the year ahead. Examine them again each year on My birthday and keep a record of the progress you have made on the path to divinity. Only in the desireless state can you reach divinity, and yet, it is within the power and grasp of each one of you to reach that state of pure bliss.

Make a new start today.

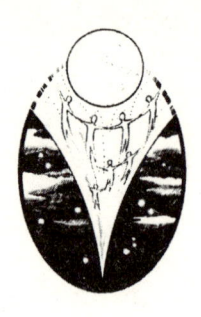

*BIRTHDAY MESSAGE NOVEMBER 1983*

## DIVINE LIFE

I am the Lord, have no doubt in your mind about that. I am the Creator of the universe. Who else do you think could have created it?

I have created everything within the universe, it is all Mine. That means it is all part of Me, for I am everywhere, in all of you and in everything. But above all these things, I am LOVE, for love is the very basis of the universe. It is this love that vibrates throughout the universe and keeps everyone and everything in a state of perfect balance. Even scientists understand this.

For Me, My birthday is your birthday, for I have taken human form for your sake. You are lucky to be here while I am here, but even that is not by accident, although few realise it. Each one of you has a unique opportunity to throw off the chains that bind you, the chains of ego, desire, and the obsession with the physical and material side of life. What are these attractions and diversions that draw you away from Me and from the love that I am pouring out into the whole universe every moment of the day like an unceasing cascade? Sadly, most of you become separated from Me and continue to chase after this and that, but what do you ever find? Perhaps, a little temporary pleasure, but what is that and how long does it last? Give up all these things, give up desire, shatter the ego, the little me that has so many wants.

Yes, My birthday is your birthday. Let it be a day of rebirth for everyone, rebirth for a new beginning, a new life full of love, full of joy and full of help and love for other people.

Try today to break with the past and let the past truly be the past. Look forward and see a new path ahead. Stick to that path which is bounded by My love on all sides. Move along that path towards liberation and ultimate bliss as you finally merge with Me.

I will help you, but you must make the effort. Being a devotee is just a beginning, like putting on a track suit before the race. But after that, effort is required, much effort, and you must stay on the track if you are going to finish the race. Are you on that track now and what effort are you really making to reach the goal, liberation?

Remember that I am always with you. I am always there to help you, but your life is in your own hands. Accept the challenge now and put into practice My teachings which you know are the truth.

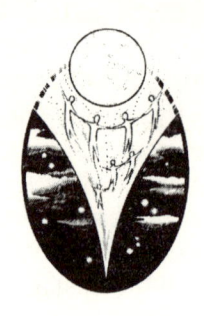

*BIRTHDAY MESSAGE NOVEMBER 1984*

## ARE YOU PROGRESSING?

**B**irthdays are days when you celebrate an aspect of creation, in this case, the birth of the Sai Avatar.

On this auspicious day you should concentrate on that form, the Sai Avatar, and contemplate exactly how you relate to Him at the present moment.

Some of you are new devotees, some have been devotees for many years, but all are My children. All are on the same path and you will only find that path through the Sai Avatar and the teachings which are now so well known.

Look back and consider what changes have taken place in your life since you found Me. Have you really changed and does your present way of life reflect an understanding of who you really are? Is the process of change continuing day by day and are you drawing closer to Me as each day passes?

Truth, Righteousness, Peace, Love and Non-Violence are what I teach, and service to fellow man, which must follow as the heart opens and you begin to treat and see others as yourself, all one, all God. So, My birthday should be a day of celebration and contemplation, the latter being more important.

I have said many times that My life is My message and you too should be able to say the same thing, that your life is your message. But you can only say this when you really live your life according to My teachings and abandon for ever more those bad habits of the past.

Let your lives be so full of love that you can be seen to be what you really are, all of you, children of the living God and beacons of Sai love and light.

It is this outpouring of Sai love and light, My love, that can save the world and bring back peace and harmony to the people in so many troubled lands.

You are the instruments and I have given each one of you this golden opportunity to work for Sai and humanity. Do not throw away that opportunity.

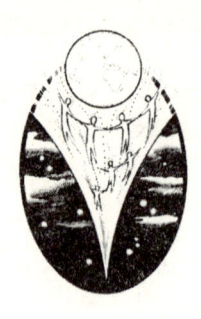

## FESTIVALS AND HOLY DAYS

**W**hy do you have festive celebrations during the year? It is an opportunity to awaken the mind of man and take his mind away from material matters and the affairs of the world. That is the true significance.

So, all festivals are for the benefit of man, not for the benefit of saints or others whose names are connected with these festivals, for they have found their own salvation.

Today should be a festival day, and tomorrow and every other day of the year. It should be your festival, the occasion when you turn to the Lord and light the candle within your own heart to illuminate your whole being, so that you may see clearly the path that leads back to God.

There is no other way, no other path, and that is why I tell you so often to open your hearts, let the love flow, and live in total harmony with God and the universe which He has created. That way you will rise up to the higher levels of consciousness where you and God really manifest as one. This is the true state of unity and divinity, the complete merging of the soul with God. That is the end of the long path which you are treading at present.

Awaken, My children, listen to the voice of God. Let His

love light up your soul and then you will see the light and hasten your journey along the path. It is within the grasp of all of you and it is only you and your material attitude to life that prevents real progress along the path.

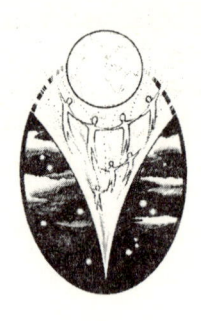

## EASWARAMMA

This is the day of the Mother and the children. And I am the Mother of each one of you and all creation. I watch over each one of you like the shepherd watching over his flock. I observe every movement, every action, every thought and, in subtle ways, I try to help you along the path. That is the duty of the mother, to bring up the children and to guide and help them as they grow up.

Where are you on that path of growing up and evolving spiritually? For that is what life is all about. Your Mother is still there, for that is Me, and I continue to watch over you with constant vigilance.

When you realise this, you should consider your own position and your responsibility in life as you grow up. Watch your words, watch your actions, watch your thoughts, watch your conscience and watch your heart. Watch all these things and try to take some definite action to improve your way of life, so that you prepare yourself for the future and shorten the journey that leads back to the Godhead.

No one can do this for you. Wiser souls can teach and guide you but, in the end, only you can take the decisions and actions to rectify the errors of the past and the present, and to prepare the way for the future.

I will always be there and will help and guide those who make the effort. But the first move must be made by you.

Start today and see how the results flow. Joy, harmony and love will become part of your life as you move along the spiritual path and leave behind the maya (illusion) of the material world and all the desires that go with it. That is what holds you back and bogs you down in a quagmire of never ending insatiable desire.

Make the decision today to cut those ties with the past, all those bad habits, and then move forward into a brighter world and a brighter, happier future, where love shines all around you like the warm rays of the sun. I will always be there waiting for you as I love you all so much.

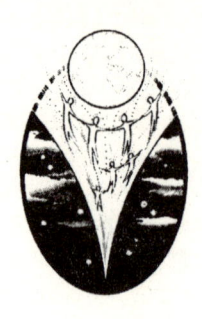

## SPIRITUAL EDUCATION

The world evolves through an unfolding and understanding of the truth and those teachers who are here today can play a part in that important process. But all teachers must first examine themselves and consider whether they are setting an example to others by their own behaviour. The end of education is character as well as knowledge, and it is character that will carry you forward along the spiritual path.

You are gathered here to listen to the message of another Teacher, the Divine Avatar, who has come into the world to save man from death and destruction, the path which man has chosen during past centuries. The transformation from that state of chaos to a spiritual one can only be achieved through education, and it is spiritual education that is the key.

So, I teach the truth in a language that anyone can understand: Truth, Righteousness, Peace, Love and Non-Violence, the corner stones of the new society which I have come to establish all over the world. All of you here today can play a part in this plan. It is up to you to take that great step forward, or continue in the wilderness, where so many people spend their lives on the earth plane, pursuing paths motivated by every aspect of desire, leading to greed, jealousy, anger and so many negative states. In such a life, man remains full of ego, thinks only about himself and his personal needs and pleasure.

My children, cast aside all such thoughts and take a great step forward today, out of the wilderness and back into the light. Start on the spiritual path which will lead you back to true happiness and a true understanding of who you really are.

All knowledge is within you now. As you change to the spiritual path, a new awakening will come to you and eventually the light will shine from within. That light is the spark of God which dwells within the heart of each one of you. Love is the source of that spark and love is the motivating force in life.

Learn to love, to love one another, and gain the understanding that you are all part of the whole, all children of the same God.

No one can claim to be a teacher until he has purified his own soul. That is the first lesson for any teacher. So study the teachings which I offer you. Then, if you put those teachings into practice you can indeed become teachers qualified to teach others less fortunate than you in this troubled world.

I am always there, watching and waiting, and I am always ready to help when you call Me and the call is from the heart.

I send My love to each one of you on the occasion of this birthday celebration, for this birthday will be your birthday if only you can understand the message and begin a new life on the true spiritual path.

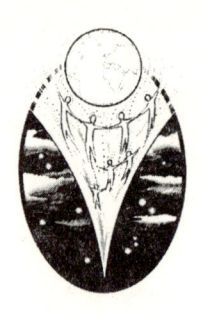

## HEALING

I am the Lord, I am you, I am the sick woman who comes to you for healing.

What are these physical symptoms from which she is suffering? They are a manifestation of separation, that is the failure of the God within to be in total harmony with the body. It is due to many causes and only you, the person, can take the steps to correct this problem, but it is not as difficult as you may think.

Once you know that all is God and there is only God, how can you continue to fear, whether it be fear of death, or failure in some worldly sense. All these things are transient including your present life on earth. So rise up to the certain knowledge that you are God, and then, what can there be to fear? God has no fears.

I will help, I will guide, and she will heal herself.

Periods of quietness to contemplate the God force are essential in these cases because only by releasing that force and allowing it to manifest in your life can peace and harmony be restored to your body and soul. It means achieving perfect harmony at all levels of consciousness.

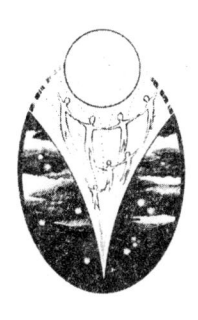

## GURU PURNIMA

Love is the starting point of all activity. Love is the foundation of the universe. Without love, life is barren and without purpose. All of you know this, but how many of you really start the day with love, spend the day with love, fill the day with love and end the day with love? Love is effervescent, like the sparkling waves of the ocean. Love brightens up everything around you. Nothing, not even evil, can stand up in the face of pure love. So, you have in your hands the solution to many of your problems, just love and surrender.

This is an important day for all of you and for Me, for I am the source of that love and I am always pouring it out in an endless stream. Today we all draw close together, so let everyone pour out that same love that I have showered upon each one of you. That love can heal and cement the relationships between everyone and especially between all members of the Sai family. It will help to eliminate all thoughts and feelings of discord or jealousy and, indeed, all negative thoughts.

I send you My blessings. Go out into the world and put My teachings into practice. Fill the world with love, My love, for without My love the world would cease to be.

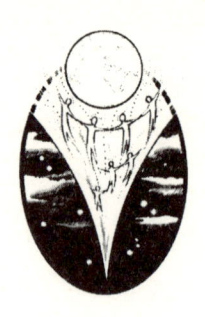

## HOLY DAY

This is a time of great celebration, for you are celebrating the birth of Christ, or the Christed One. This is, indeed, a divine day and a divine occasion. It is also an important day for each one of you as, on this auspicious day, you should examine yourself to see what point you have reached on the long road that leads to divinity.

Celebrations are good, but the best celebration will take place when you realise your inherent divinity and live your life manifesting as a truly divine soul or being. There are very few people on earth who can claim to be doing this. Why is that? It results from the temptations all around you and the constant desire of the lower aspects of man. You must learn to overcome these weaknesses, remembering that they are there for a purpose. It is the experience of the lower aspects, and the ultimate realisation of the utter impossibility of achieving peace of mind through attachment to such things, that eventually leads man out of the wilderness and onto the spiritual path.

Over and over again, I tell you these things because it is only through constant repetition that My message will be understood. Only My teachings can bring about the changes in man and lead him from a state of misery to ultimate bliss. It is a long and arduous path, but all will reach the destination in the end. So, examine your lives on this auspicious day and start to bring about the changes which you know within are essential for your future progress and happiness. Throw off those chains that bind you and break away for ever from the past and the failures that accompanied it.

I come to awaken the hearts of men and to help them realise the divinity within. It is there, it is there, within you now, if only you could know it. Live in that divine state NOW and give up for ever all attachment and earthly desires. That will truly make Me very happy.

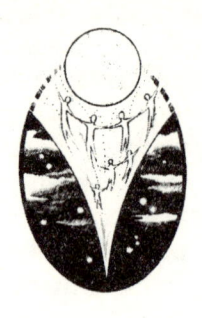

## LOVING GOD

These meetings [of Sai groups] are a gathering of like minds, occasions when the love of God can flow freely and cleanse the atmosphere all around you.

It is the thought process that matters. When you meet together, all is positive, all are in tune, vibrations of love are created and it is these vibrations that affect the surroundings.

Progress in these Sai groups has been encouraging and it is the best way to spread the word of Sai in the western world. People will be drawn to these groups when they are ready and others will be guided towards them after much searching.

Man searches for God and those who eventually find God do so through their own awakening and the realisation that God dwells within. For within and without, all is God. He is omnipresent, here, there and everywhere, and yet, man can spend a whole lifetime searching for God, even in the Himalayas, and yet God is there beside him, within him, around him all the time.

Even when you find God dwelling in your heart, that discovery alone leads you nowhere unless you establish a relationship with Him, a relationship which leads to the realisation that you and He are one. "I am you, you are Me, all one, all God." Those are words which you have heard from the lips of the Sai Avatar. Those words were not spoken without purpose and you should dwell on them and let the whole world become aware of this fundamental truth.

Live in love, live in God, live with God, live with the certain knowledge that you and God are one, all part of the whole. See God in everyone, everywhere, only then can you throw away the cares of the world and find peace, harmony and tranquillity. For without these qualities it will be difficult to make any real progress on the spiritual path.

Love one another, that is the starting point of every spiritual journey.

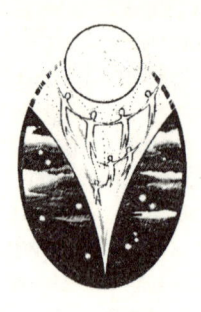

## OMNIPRESENCE OF GOD
### (AND MAN'S FREE WILL)

My child, I reside in the heart of man and at this moment I give you this message. It is a message of love, a manifestation of the divinity that pervades the universe.

God is here, God is there, God is everywhere, God is in all and in everything.

If this is true, and it is true, there should be perfect unity and harmony throughout the universe. But on earth it is not so. Why is that? Why is love absent? Why is there so little unity and harmony?

It is because I have created man with free will, and man has chosen to play out a life separated, as far as he can be, from God, even though God still resides in his heart.

This is God's game, life on earth with that freedom of will, an exercise to demonstrate that there is only God and that life without God is not only illusion but completely barren.

It is a game, but it has a deep purpose, and one day man will be reawakened and the game will come to an end. That awakening is happening now and many will find the way back to God, that is, living in perfect harmony with God, knowing that in truth there is only God and that all is God.

It is through the experience of illusion that man becomes awakened and the whole process is part of God's plan for evolution.

Never doubt the truth of what I tell you. Remember the words of God, remember the name of God, remember that God is love, then peace and harmony will return to your life.

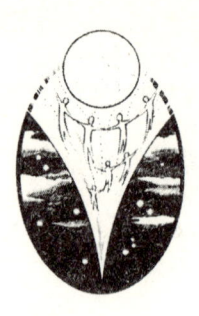

## PEACE

Glorious is life in the presence of the Lord. All earthly thoughts merge with the divine and all worries dissolve, for the Lord has no worries. Then the sun shines incessantly as a glowing flame within the heart and illumines the whole being and the world around.

Can you imagine a whole crowd of people, all perfectly attuned to divinity, all glowing within and without? It is a state of ecstasy when you can truly say I AM.

Love must flow incessantly for love is the life force, the sustainer of the whole universe.

What problem can possibly remain if you follow the teachings of the Lord?

Contemplate these thoughts and try to follow in the divine footsteps until you and God are one. Then peace, happiness, tranquillity and contentment will replace the worries of daily life; and all doubts and fears will cease to be.

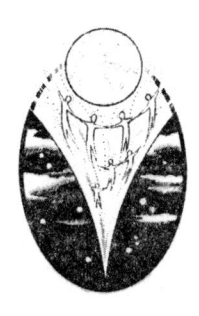

## PRESENCE OF GOD

**S**wami is omnipresent and is here with you now. Omnipresence is something which may be difficult for some of you to understand, but it means I am with each one of you all the time, every moment of your lives, hence I know every thought you have ever had. Few of you bother to make use of this omnipresence or are even aware of it. If you can learn to bring me into your lives, then slowly, you will begin to reap the benefits from an awareness of the God within.

You spend so much of your time worrying about petty problems, but most of these are here today and gone tomorrow. What is their importance in the eternal life? Offer your problems to Me and see what a difference it makes when you bring Me into your lives. Have no fear of life, for it is like a playground where you gain certain experiences. Use this time to prepare yourselves for the eternal life that lies ahead. As I have often said, "Why fear when I am here?"

Remember the teachings of Christ, for these same teachings are what I am teaching today. Remember above all things that God is love and learn to love one another. Remember what I told you the other day, when you asked how you could help Swami. BE LIKE A BEACON IN THE SKY, RADIATING LOVE AND LIGHT. Those remarks apply to all of you.

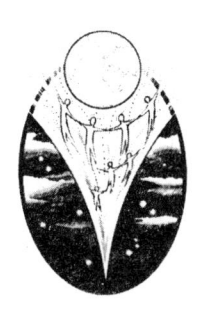

## THE DIVINE SPRING

It is good that you spread the word of the Lord, for now is the time of awakening for your planet and all those who reside there. The days of darkness are drawing to a close and the shadows lengthening until they disappear, to be replaced by brilliant sunshine, so strong that it will cleanse the planet and leave it ready for a new golden era.

Some are ready, some are not. Those who are ready will be drawn to the Sai groups that will be formed all over the world. They will spring up naturally because I will call the people and organise them, even though they may think that they are doing it themselves.

There will be many wondrous signs to show the presence of the Lord in all these plans and developments.

You all have important parts to play, so simply continue as you are doing, and let the flowers spring up all around you. I am in every one of those flowers for I am the light and will show you the way.

God does not reveal all His plans in advance, the mystery of the Lord will always remain.

Fear not, My children, all will be well. Love and light will replace the darkness and a new era will be upon you very soon.

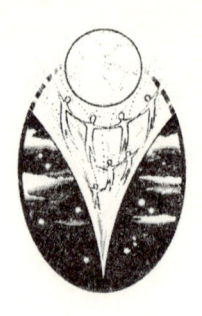

## THE NIGHT OF SHIVA'S MOON

What is Shivaratri? It is the opening up of fresh thoughts in preparation for the year ahead. These occasions should be ones of deep meditation, an opportunity to look deep inside yourselves, to look at the real position within, the state of your soul and its progress on the spiritual path. It is a time of decision, a time and opportunity for a new move forward onto a better path. That is what I ask each one of you to do every day!

You sit, you listen, you read My teachings. What is the good, unless you put these teachings into practice?

I watch every movement, every thought, every action of yours. You should do the same and constantly ask yourselves if these thoughts and actions are based on the teachings of the Lord. They are not! But today is yet another day of opportunity, a chance to make that new start on the only path that can lead to true divinity and eventual liberation from the chains that bind you to constant rebirth in the physical body. Those chains are desire, unfulfilled desire, desire for all that is transient, unnecessary and unfulfilling.

Man must overcome desire and turn to love because, if you fill your heart with the love of God, your desire for material things and sensual pleasures will slowly fall away.

I am always with you, always there to help and guide, but only you can take the decision to change your own way of life and break those habits that lead you astray.

Life spiritual is God. Life material is illusion.

Make the choice today to see the light and live your life from now on in perfect harmony with the Lord.

Liberation may take time to achieve, but peace will come to your minds as soon as you put your feet, and your heart, on the true spiritual path.

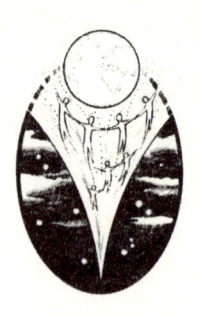

## THE UNITY OF GOD'S WAY

Co-operation results from an expanding heart. Where there is none, it is due to a failure to open the heart, and it means that the animal instincts remain in the ascendant. Thus, the ego remains strong, and with it desire. Against such a background, the will to co-operate does not come easily.

Look at your own Sai organisation. Why is it unsatisfactory? There are factions here, factions there. Half of them do not really know what they want, except only that they do not wish to co-operate. It is a form of protest and shows the true state of their souls. But one must try to help them, find out what they want and try to bring them back into the fold to be part of the whole.

I have said many times that there is no unity in your country and it is so. All these cliques, petty squabbles, even among people in high positions. No one seems to have reached a full understanding of My message and few people reflect the love which I have showered upon them. They are separated, isolated, and they try to continue their own lives along the same old lines, but this will lead them nowhere. Even those who visit Me are little better. They come, they go, but what happens? They simply return to their old habits and their old way of life and make no real effort to put My teachings into practice.

But change will come. The day of awakening is not so far away and when it comes there will be a revelation of the true power of God, a manifestation of the omnipresence of the Lord. This will be the signal for a great move forward and the weeding out of those who are not ready to accept the challenge of the moment. It will be just so, mark My words. But few will listen, very few.

After the storm there will be a new beginning and the atmosphere will be completely different. It will be like a new age, the age of love, harmony and co-operation replacing the age of war, fighting, hatred, jealousy, greed and all those negative aspects of life. Everyone should prepare NOW for this change, for I promise you that it will come, and only those who are ready will survive.

I have given the warning, I have given My message a thousand times and no one who hears My words can claim ignorance. Do not delay action to put right your own life style and to change it to the way of God. There is no other way.

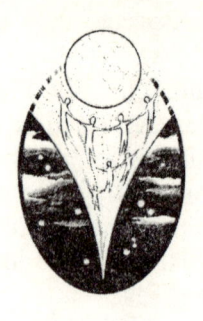

## SAIDAY

**W**hy do you gather here for My birthday, dear children? Is it to see the light? Some of you have seen the light; others are aware that the light exists and know they must find it and follow the only path that will lead them back to divinity and the ultimate merging of the soul with the Lord. I am that light and I am everywhere. I am here as you read these words. Just pause for a few moments and try to feel and experience My omnipresence.

This is the secret, the mystery of life: to experience the omnipresence of the Lord, for it brings with it the opening to a new life, that is, a life in the infinite presence of the Lord. In that state the Lord takes care of you and your whole life. It is the choice of a life in isolation and obscurity, or life in the everlasting presence of the Lord. You have that choice and only you can bring about the change.

Meditate on these thoughts, talk to the Lord at every opportunity during the day, and then He will come to you. Become aware of His presence everywhere, in everyone and everything, and the fact that in reality there is only God. All other thoughts are a form of illusion.

Love is the path to God for true love is God. Bring love into your lives, love one another and then you will prepare the way for God to walk beside you on the long journey that leads back to the divine state.

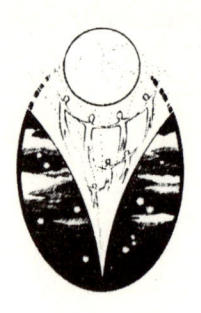

## WHAT CAN I DO FOR YOU, LORD?

Be like a beacon in the sky, radiating love and light, that is what you can do for Swami. Do not worry about what other people think of you or try to please them. If you radiate love and light, all problems, great and small, will simply dissolve. It is the best solution for all your problems. Do not get angry or upset, that means giving in to negative forces. When unpleasantness is directed against you, return love and light, for nothing can stand up when confronted by pure love and light.

# INDEX

## Part I  LOVE                                             1

| | |
|---|---|
| Love is the message | 3 |
| Love is the very basis | 5 |
| Devotion and love flow | 7 |
| My love is like a mountain | 9 |
| Love flows when you gather | 10 |
| Love is the foundation | 12 |
| Love leads to unity | 14 |
| Unity and love | 15 |
| My love surrounds you | 17 |
| On this lovely early morning | 19 |
| Talk to them | 21 |
| Why do you worry | 22 |
| There is calm | 24 |
| When love flows from the heart | 25 |
| When you gather together | 26 |
| Swami's life is | 27 |
| I am LOVE | 29 |

## Part II  OTHER THEMES                                   33

| | |
|---|---|
| Aim of Life, The | 104 |
| Being | 100 |
| Birthday Message, November 1982, Birth Day | 118 |
| Birthday Message, November 1983, Divine Life | 120 |
| Birthday Message, November 1984, Are You Progressing? | 122 |
| Christmas Message, 1983 | 108 |
| Christmas Message, 1984 | 110 |
| Christmas Message for the Sai Children, A | 106 |
| Confidence | 94 |
| Contemplating the Truth | 71 |
| Courage | 114 |
| Creation | 90 |
| Creator, Creature and Creation | 83 |

| | |
|---|---|
| Depression | 48 |
| Divine Design | 98 |
| Divine Spring, The | 141 |
| Easwaramma | 126 |
| Education in Human Values | 112 |
| Effort | 102 |
| Facing up to Life's Difficulties | 42 |
| Faith | 116 |
| Festivals and Holy Days | 124 |
| Food for the Lord | 50 |
| Freedom | 37 |
| Free Will | 52 |
| God and Religion | 55 |
| Guru Purnima | 131 |
| Healing | 130 |
| Holy Day | 132 |
| Inner Control | 69 |
| Inner Teacher, The | 77 |
| Inner Voice, The | 63 |
| Levels of Consciousness | 88 |
| Life Without Love | 35 |
| Loving God | 134 |
| Man's Identity | 57 |
| Negative Feelings | 39 |
| New Year (1983) | 117 |
| Night of Shiva's Moon, The | 142 |
| Obstacles | 44 |
| Omnipresence | 67 |
| Omnipresence of God | 136 |
| Peace | 138 |
| Presence of God | 139 |
| Saiday | 146 |
| Sai Mission, The | 61 |
| Sai Organisation, The | 72 |
| Security and Insecurity | 40 |
| Spiritual Education | 128 |
| Spiritual Effort (I) | 59 |
| Spiritual Effort (II) | 73 |

| | |
|---|---|
| Surrender (I) | 65 |
| Surrender (II) | 75 |
| Time (I) | 79 |
| Time (II) | 81 |
| Unity (I) | 53 |
| Unity (II) | 86 |
| Unity (III) | 92 |
| Unity (IV) | 96 |
| Unity in Action | 85 |
| Unity of God's Way, The | 144 |
| Violence in the World | 46 |
| What Can I Do for You, Lord? | 148 |